GUIDE
TO
I CHING

GUIDE
TO
I CHING

Raymond R Bullock

CAXTON REFERENCE

© 2000 Caxton Editions

This edition published 2000 by Caxton Editions,
20 Bloomsbury Street, London, WC1B 3QA.

Caxton Editions is an imprint of the Caxton Publishing Group.

Printed and bound in India.

ABOUT THE AUTHOR

Raymond R Bullock is a poet and writer from the Wirral, currently teaching T'ai Ji Quan and martial arts, as well as Oriental poetry. He also promotes group studies in stress reduction through contemplative writing and T'ai Ji exercises.

After studying at John Moores University in Liverpool he received a degree in Philosophy and Imaginative Writing and a Master's degree in Writing.

His interest in Chinese philosophy and related arts ranges over a thirty-year period, and centres around the study of the I Ching and its use as an instrument in self-development.

Writing interests at the present time include, a Guide to the Art of Strategy, a compilation of poetry and photographic images, and a study of stress reduction through T'ai Ji Quan and related exercises.

CONTENTS

Some misquotes from Gary Zukav's *The Dancing Wu Li Masters.*

> *The master always teaches from the centre...*
> > *he teaches essence.*
> *Whatever he does, he does with the enthusiasm of*
> > *doing it for the first time.*

My thanks to those instructors who understood how to apply this art, primarily Vinny H, for his illimitable patience and direction.

Dr. Edmund Cusack of JM. for support and understanding above and beyond...and to my T'ai Ji instructor Master Kam Lau

Thanks also to those authors to be found in the bibliography, whose texts have deepened my understanding and made the writing of this simple guide possible.

INTRODUCTION

History of the I Ching

The original texts of the I Ching, commonly translated as the Book of Changes, is credited to Fu Hsi the first Chinese Emperor, in or around 3000 BC. As well as devising the 64 hexagrams and developing the beginnings of Chinese culture and society, he is believed to have taught animal husbandry, fishing and hunting skills to his subjects.

In approximately 1150 BC a popular feudal lord from the West of China by the name of Wen, was imprisoned by the Shang Emperor. During his imprisonment he composed a set of judgements to the hexagrams.

After the overthrow of the Emperor and his release, his son added interpretations to the individual lines. His son the duke of Chou, became the founder of the Chou dynasty, and posthumously bestowed the title of king upon his father. The book at this time was called the Chou I, or Change of Chou.

Confucius is reputed to have added commentaries after many years of study, in the fifth century BC, though in modern times doubts have been raised whether it was he or his followers who wrote these. What is known is that the book was greatly increased, in size and content, as a result of Confucian thought, and soon became known as a Confucian Classic under its present name, the I Ching.

Throughout Chinese history great philosophers, alchemists, magicians and mystics have used and translated the I Ching into their own beliefs. *The Art of War* written by Sun Tsu, has its origins in the Book of Changes as does the Taoist exercise system of T'ai Ji Quan. Its inventor Chang San-feng laid great emphasis on the superior or true mind, in contrast to the conditioned or human mind. He formulated the T'ai Ji Quan exercise in order to balance the yin and yang elements, and allow the superior mind to direct the consciousness, and the vital energy.

Sage-Kings

Men who had uncommon knowledge, who knew the hidden springs of the future, composed the set of writings known today as the I Ching. This means that they could discern the first indications of change, that they could clearly differentiate the real from the false. These men were the sage-kings of antiquity, who possessed spiritual power but lived in the world: they understood the Tao (the Way) of transformation and the nature of heaven and earth. They lived neither in seclusion nor endless meditation, though they employed both of these exercises when necessary, rather they spent their lives as teachers.

They believed that character represented the image of God in man, and was therefore the superior self; that personality was the seat of the ego and instinctive drives, and therefore the lower self; that harmony could be achieved when each performed its proper function, according to the nature heaven had assigned to it.

Character expansion then, involved sacrificing selfishness (self-centredness), and this required positive action. The foundation of character was proper conduct, and could be extended through self-examination and an enduring attitude. Reducing instincts and increasing the scope of character could bring about acceptance in oppressive situations, rather than resentment and despair. Finally, growth of character would depend on effective work with others, and an attitude, which was both humble and flexible.

These of course were all great men: men of superior moral intelligence, gifted with phenomenal insight: so of what use are the intuitions of such men to ordinary people such as ourselves? In the paragraph above I give a brief sketch, of the guidelines for the formation of character, as represented by nine of the hexagrams in the Book of Changes.

The next question then, even supposing we are willing to attempt such a program, is how? How can we act properly – in all circumstances? How do we practice self-examination, or keep an enduring attitude? How do we reduce instincts, increase the scope of character, and accept all situations equally? All this and be humble and flexible with other people at the same time? Such an impossible task is fine for saints and superior men, we say, but not for us. This is probably true, if we think that self-improvement is about comfort and self-esteem, but if having read this far there is still a hunger to know more, then the I Ching might be for you.

The main obstacle to finding a correct way to live, for most people, is that they lack good teaching. Or if they are persevering, and find a good teacher, the program itself might be too extreme, or too mild. The list of obstacles might go on forever, but what is certain is that they will remain until we make a beginning, and this beginning must be simple and easy.

When we think of learning, it usually comprises of a difficult course of study, resulting in a practical increase in our store of knowledge: knowledge we can manipulate, adding or taking away as required. This system works for many of the practical and impersonal aspects of our lives, but when philosophical and moral teaching are insufficient, what we require is a means to a higher level of understanding. This is where the I Ching comes in.

The I Ching is a text much used by the Taoists: Tao meaning The Way, and comprising of universal and particular principles. Through the use of the I Ching, Chinese thinkers sought to understand the true nature of, and the connections between, mankind and the cosmos. More specifically they sought to awaken the human potential formerly blocked by conditioning. Rational thinking, instinct and ego, important faculties in their own spheres, were the main authors of this conditioning they decided: the I Ching was their main avenue out of the morass.

Meditation and periods of isolation were important exercises in breaking the bonds of habit, but the finest exercise was to find inner quietness while in the midst of outer disturbance. If the nature of the inner (subjective) disturbance was known, for example emotionally charged reactions, or obsessive attitudes, then they could be removed from an objective standpoint.

The purpose of the I Ching is to point the way towards a new attitude by dissolving the old one. This is done via the individual lines (of the hexagrams), representing in a general way, difficulties at different levels of experience. (For explanation of the lines read the chapter, CONSULTING THE ORACLE).

Simply put, the six lines of each hexagram represent the old restrictive point of view, conditioned by personality, and at the same time, suggest a more detached attitude toward the situation. It is through this attitude of open-minded awareness that the individual changes come about.

When the individual changes are manifest, the view changes: we have entered the new dimension of being. Habitual thinking will always draw us back, as we enter into further situations, but this is the nature of change: for character to increase there needs to be a decrease in personality – old patterns of behaviour sacrificed, in favour of the wider and clearer viewpoint.

The above is of course a much simplified version of the workings of the I Ching. It does not take into account, for example, the image of the hexagram as a whole, or the energy represented by the trigrams and their symbolism. Also each change has its own time, and therefore cannot be instigated by self-will. All of these can be explained in more depth later; for the moment we need only investigate the actions of the book, from the viewpoint of our own personal requirements.

Many of us, with a desire to alter our lives, have a vague notion that changes depend on strength of will. This delusory attitude usually results in extremist behaviour rituals, in which we make greater and greater demands on the will, or become ever more dependent on our failures. Dilemmas such as these grow out of ignorance of natural laws, and over-dependence on conditioned thinking, and consequently lead us away from change.

The I Ching deals directly with changes: non-change, cyclic and sequential change.

Non-change is the T'ai Chi or Ultimate Point of Perfection, which we can interpret as our Ideal. To broaden this concept of non-change, we might also think of Ideal as implying potential. From this point of reference, the Ideal through its potential enters into the world in the form of yin and yang, the positive and negative elements of the universe. These elements are symbolised in the hexagrams of Heaven and Earth, corresponding with the higher and lower natures of mankind.

Higher refers to spirit, yang, and character, whereas lower depicts temporal, yin, and personality. So, the terms higher and lower present the relationship between the governing forces of heaven, and the dependent forces of earth, as interrelated, harmonious opposites. Metaphorically, there is a kind of dove-tailing, which benefits both forces.

The energy of heaven, as revealed in the movements of celestial bodies represents constant change through definable, rather than chaotic, laws. These same laws bind the world, and so we can predict the change of seasons, day and night and the months of the year: this is the phenomenon we call time, and represents cyclic or recurrent change.

Sequential change describes progressive transformation. In I Ching terms this is called cause and effect.

The Creative and Receptive hexagrams depict perfect yin and yang, symbolising the Mother and Father principles; their primary attributes of flexibility and firmness; and the correct or incorrect use of energies, according to their proper time.

The other sixty-two hexagrams depict aspects of practical experience, in the form of images, whose individual lines suggest the attitude and action to be taken or avoided, and whether this will lead to good or ill fortune. What this means is that, having identified change in its minute beginnings, we can if we choose forestall misfortune in our lives.

What we must remember here is that misfortune means only that the course of action is not in harmony with the laws of heaven, and therefore contrary to our true natures. If we continue in the wrong direction for a period of time and then, through remorse, redirect our actions, we will secure good fortune for ourselves.

The important point is that good fortune, for the book of changes, means following our true natures and therefore, the will of heaven. It seems obvious then that if we continue to follow the wrong course regardless of our fate, or if we slip from the correct path arrogantly denying the outcome, then we must eventually suffer humiliations, until we can again find the right path.

A further point to remember, is that the purpose of the I Ching is to broaden the outlook by the removal of destructive attitudes: perspectives that represent the accumulation of conditioned reactions and behaviour patterns, and are firmly attached to our personal defence system.

It is these destructive elements of our personalities
that stand in the way of personal fulfilment, and so
only these that need to be eliminated, or where
possible, transformed into a positive characteristic,
more favourable to the attainment of our fullest
potential. Practical illustrations of destructive
attitudes would be worthwhile at this stage, and might
run something like the following:

Recognising that a failing relationship is caused by
dependency, we become self-assertive, or in detecting
certain weaknesses, develop aggressive tendencies. We
could make endless lists of defective reactions, but
these will do for our demonstration.

If we look at our illustration objectively, we can
see that the solution to the failure of one extreme is to
project the will through its opposite: or what is
perceived as the opposite. The obvious difficulty with
such a solution is that it is a closed system: either this
or that. Less obvious is the fact that it is based on
failure i.e. the move to self-assertion being a move
away from dependency. This must result in a
succession of failures, because both are really
extremes of the same problem: the desire to achieve
satisfaction by making demands on others.

To achieve real satisfaction in our lives, we must
first make use of all of our attributes, but again, our
closed system makes this impossible. To alter our
viewpoint requires that, for a moment at least, we
must give up the old one – completely. Why – because
we cannot squeeze a new point of view into a closed

system.

In using the I Ching, we step out of the old system the moment we throw the coins; then into the new one as we follow the suggestions of the reading. If we do this each time the old strategy fails us, and continue with our efforts, however limited they might seem, it will eventually become clear that we have entered a further stage in our development: that we are expanding our characters, from the point of view of character. It is this further dimension of being, this unrestricted consciousness, which was the primary quality of the sages of the past.

'Of what use', we asked, 'are the intuitions of such men to ordinary people like ourselves?' I hope that the opening part of this introduction will go some way to answering that question.

Teachings of the Sage-Kings

The primary purpose of the sages, the 'men of old', was to teach simple skills. They knew that, 'real and practical knowledge' that has any worth, is taught at the moment of experience. The book of changes was formulated to teach in precisely this way. Here is a system of self-improvement to be used when required, at an easy pace. Like the water in a well, it is there when needed, to be used by everyone.

Water is fundamental to all life, in the same way that spiritual nourishment fulfils the basic needs of societies and individuals. To be worth anything, a system of self-development must be available to everyone, whatever their nature or education, and should employ a simple and easy method of obtaining full potential. Such a transformation should also include the ability to teach what has been learned.

What the book offers, as a representative of those who formulated its text over millenia, is the ability to make gradual progress toward a point of view beyond what we can imagine. Secondly, to consolidate this attitude by awakening intuitive skills and insights, and finally to expand our perspective daily, by regular use of what we learn by freely teaching it to others. In short and unlikely as it seems, to become like them.

The terms, sage and sage-king are much used in the commentary of the hexagrams, as also are central character, ruler, leader, man of character etc. These all refer to the person who has become spiritually centred by entering this further dimension of being, and whose duty it is to pass on the teaching to others.

Chinese philosophy explains the obligation of the sage-king as, 'one who freely functions in society, while aspiring to the truth of the spirit.'

Philosophy of the I Ching
In this philosophy terms such as yin/yang, receptive/ creative, yielding/ strength, instinct/intuition, personality/character, physical/spiritual, and many more are descriptions of complimentary opposites and their relationships.

The harmonising of these energies and qualities, and the overall effect this has on human life, is the primary purpose of this philosophy. Its objective is the ability to function freely in the world in a practical sense, while remaining in this further dimension of being, in a spiritual sense.

For an example of this integration we can use the complimentary opposites of movement and rest:

Peace of mind (resting within) while performing everyday tasks (movement) is the result of quieting the will (active thought patterns). This quieting process is brought about by actively examining the habits of mind. Applying this examination process correctly i.e. objectively decreases the energy of the obsessive thought patterns.

Paradoxically then, the way to remove active obsessions is through accepting we cannot remove them. This is called action through inaction.

The above depicts the manner in which rest and movement work together to complete themselves, meaning that they are in harmony. Also implied is that the nature of obsession is, 'habitually returning to the same destructive patterns of thought and action', and for this lack of clarity we might also use the term insanity.

Whether or not we agree with the above definition, we ought to investigate the I Ching's interpretation of sanity, and how such a quality can be achieved.

The Transformation Process

We have noted that the primary hexagrams, the Creative and Receptive refer to complimentary opposites, in the form of energy, interdependent upon one another. The energy of heaven (the Creative) and the energy of earth (the Receptive) intermingle, and produce all living things. This renewal of life is manifest through the passage of the seasons, and the coming and going of day and night.

This refers to the waxing and waning of yin and yang or the tao (way) of transformation. Yang denotes the active energy in the production of living things, and yin, the passive or receptive energy. In this process yin and yang intermingle, while persisting in their natures, and reach a point of completion. The meaning of completion is simply that things have attained their proper condition in their proper time.

This process, resulting in completion, also applies to experience: therefore when our energies are balanced i.e. in harmony with Heaven and Earth, it can be said that we have become receptive to reality. Being receptive to reality is perceived as that supreme quality called sanity.

Summary

The I Ching was composed by sage-kings over thousands of years, and is the foundation of Chinese culture and thought. 'Sage-kings' is the term for those people who have attained enlightenment, yet retain a practical function in the world. The primary expression of this function is continuous spiritual growth, through freely teaching others. The I Ching is the text of this teaching, through which others can transcend the limits of personality, and enter this further dimension of existence.

The primary hexagrams of the Creative (yang) and the Receptive (yin) represent Heaven and Earth, male/female, firmness/flexibility,character/personality complimentary opposites whose forces intertwine in a never-ending stream of transformation.

Good fortune represents aligning with the true nature of things – with the Will of Heaven. Misfortune occurs when we follow the wrong course, or ignore the correct time for change. Humiliation depicts a condition of stubborn resistance to change. These delusory attitudes we have called insanity.

Achieving a new standpoint founded on formation of character (the higher self,) and sacrifice of personality (lower self). This clear view of reality we call sanity.

The next chapter deals with technical information, with definition of the hexagrams, trigrams and lines, and the use of the book as an oracle and book of wisdom.

Hexagrams

The sixty-four hexagrams and three hundred and eighty-four yao (individual lines that make up each hexagram) each symbolise an event in time and space. The accompanying interpretations suggest the correct course of action for the time and circumstance. Because each hexagram represents an image of the whole event, and the lines offer specific directions with regard to the changes we need to make, complex problems become simple and easy to overcome. Therefore, at the centre of complexities the I Ching reveals simplicity. The Creative is easy to know – the receptive simple to apply. When the simple and easy combine, all transformations are predictable.

Each one of the hexagrams deals with more than one group of things, while the commentaries attached translate the symbolic meaning of each of these groups. Therefore there can be no fixed interpretation, because the translation alters to fit the situation of the time, and the condition of the individual seeking guidance.

The sages observed the phenomena in the heavens and the world, and found the representations of these in mankind. Through the formulation and use of the I Ching, these complex patterns could be reduced to simple principles by which a way could be found through the apparent chaos.

The T'ai Chi

In understanding the connections between man his world and the cosmos, the unceasing confusion and sense of isolation is removed from the individual. This understanding, this knowledge of the true self, is the first step in the transformation process.

This process we can define in the form of a lineage as follows:

The I Ching consists of the T'ai Chi (the Great Ultimate) as expressed through yin and yang, and the two stages of each of these (Greater and Lesser yin and yang; see below). From these grew the eight trigrams from which good fortune and misfortune could be known, and finally the hexagrams by which mankind could achieve greatness through transformation.

In Chinese philosophy, the unchanging, the T'ai Chi (chi meaning ridgepole) is the symbol of Oneness and represented by a single unbroken line (———).

From this came the simple idea of above and below, the above still characterising that which is unchanging, while below symbolising that which could be changed. This is represented by a broken line, as something waiting to be filled up (— —). These came to stand for the primary forces of light and dark, which when doubled like so

Greater Yang	Greater Yin	Lesser Yang	Lesser Yin
———	— —	— —	———
———	— —	———	— —

represented the transformations consistent with the four seasons. (For further information read the chapter on trigrams, and the commentaries for the hexagrams)

In the chapter for the sixty-four hexagrams I have given the number of the hexagram, its Chinese name and English translation, followed by the names and positions of the trigrams, which make up the hexagram. Certain qualities and aphorisms follow.

After these come a simple commentary, the judgement, image and interpretations of the lines. In compiling these I have used a variety of reference material, primarily the Richard Wilhelm translation, the list of which can be found in the bibliography.

Lines

The six lines that make up each hexagram are yin or yang, firm or flexible. These lines can change to their opposite under certain conditions- yin to yang and yang to yin. This transformation of one principle to another is called moving. Lines that move signify an alteration in the situation as a whole, which is then defined by the new hexagram. (See Consulting the Oracle) When there are none of these moving lines, then the hexagram is viewed as resting i.e. unchanging: the situation as a whole is not at the point of transformation, and we should refer to the hexagram only for information concerning our present condition.

The individual lines are classified in the following way: bottom and top lines are perceived as out of the situation. The lowest line is often seen as the place where the first movements become manifest, though the counsel is quite often to wait for a better time. The upper line is for the sage who has evolved beyond worldly interests. This place is sometimes personified by the egoist personality, who has over-extended himself.

The even numbered lines inside the hexagram are yin and usually characterised by officials, sons or women. Of these the fourth takes the superior position, being the place of the minister, priest or mediator. The second position is for the servant, or follower of the central character.

The odd numbered lines are yang, and in places of

authority. The third line, because it leads the lower trigram and the fifth line because it rules the whole hexagram. This is the central character, the sage/teacher.

The terms 'superior and inferior' with regard to the lines depends on their position within the hexagram i.e. lines in the lower trigram being inferior to those above. This exemplifies the standpoint of the teaching, which is that the upper trigram represents character or spirit, whereas the lower represents personality in the form of instincts etc.

Remember that the hexagrams are built from the bottom upwards.

The first (bottom) and last (top) lines represent cause and effect, respectively, being outside of the action. The bottom line is the first manifestation of change; the last is the end result.

The fifth line rules the hexagram with the second and fourth lines as officials. The second line corresponds directly with the fifth, being the central line of the lower trigram. Figuratively this might mean the ruler's representative in distant parts, or that what is represented is a practical manifestation of a spiritual ideal. The fourth line transmits the will of the ruler to the people (the other lines), or the spiritual message of the central character as it applies to the situation. The second line is usually favourable while the fourth quite often receives a warning. The fifth line is the central place in the hexagram and depicts the ruler of the state. It also stands in place of

the sage, the central character, spiritual man etc.
Finally it represents the seat of character within the
individual. The third line is at the top of the lower
trigram, and being yang is active. It usually suffers
from much insecurity because it relies on instincts
and desires for its motivation.

As well as correspondence between the second
and fifth lines, there is correspondence between the
first and fourth, and the third and sixth.

Odd numbered places one, three and five are
favourably yang, even numbered are favourably yin.
The term yielding (for yin), depicts the proper
attitude toward the ruler.

The hexagram is also divided into three parts to
represent the primal energies of earth, man and
heaven. The two lower lines for earth, the top two for
heaven, with the middle lines for mankind.

Trigrams

The hexagrams are also made of two groups of three
lines, called trigrams. There are eight of these, and
their various combinations form the sixty-four
hexagrams.

Heaven	Earth	Fire	Water
Thunder	Mountain	Lake	Wind/wood

The eight trigrams are shown on the previous page.
   The attributes, images and family structure that
represent the trigrams is as follows:

- Heaven is Creative in its will, is strong and
  firm and represents the father.

- Earth is Receptive and flexible and represents the
  mother.

- Fire is clinging, illuminates and represents the
  spirit and the middle daughter.

- Water is abysmal and dangerous, the vital energy
  and middle son.

- Thunder has power to animate, is the voice of
  God, and the first son.

- Wind (and wood) is gentleness, penetrating and
  the first daughter.

- Mountain is stillness, meditation and the youngest
  son.

- The Lake is joyful living, pleasure and the
  youngest daughter.

   A sequence of the trigrams representing their
manifestation in the yearly cycle, credited to King
Wen, is called the Inner-world Arrangement. This
arrangement portrays the manifestation of the divine
in nature:

> God speaks (awakens or rouses) things through thunder; completes things through the gentleness of wind; creates awareness through the illumination of fire- service through the receptivity of Earth. He makes joy to rise from the depths of the lake- He combats evil in the power of the Creative- to make work possible he creates the vital energy symbolised by water, and makes things perfect (rich) in the stillness of the mountain.

Continuing with the theme of the manifestation of the spirit, as it appears in the world, each trigram is given a direction i.e. space, and a time in the year:

> Thunder awakens life in spring and the East.
> Wind completes things at the end of spring, in the southeast.
> Fire illuminates in summer and the south, and living things become aware of each other.
> Earth teaches all things to nourish each other in the southwest, at the end of Summer.
> In Autumn all things are joyous in the west.
> The Creative combats dark forces in the northwest.
> In the north all life works through the Winter months through the vital energies of water.
> In the northeast the image of the mountain, at winter's end symbolising the perfection of life.

The same sequence would apply for the twenty-four hour daily cycle:

Thunder is morning; Wind/Wood- mid-morning; Fire is midday; Earth is mid-afternoon; the Lake is evening; Heaven is sunset; Water, the abysmal is mid-night. Mountain, as in the cycle of the year, represents the end and beginning, the last moments of night, as the light of the sun begins to appear over distant hills.

Symbolic animals for the trigrams are as follows:
The Creative is the dragon, the Receptive is the mare, Gentleness is the cockerel, Abysmal is the pig, the Clinging is the firebird, Stillness the dog and Joyousness the goat.

There are many more symbols for each of the trigrams, but the above lists are sufficient for this simple guide. It is important however to have an understanding of why the various symbols apply, and for this we will investigate the nature of the animals in the above list to see where they correspond with the trigrams they represent.

If for instance we ask why the dragon stands for the Creative power, we should look for the symbolic nature of the dragon. This mythical beast symbolises the power that shapes the galaxies, or in the world it is Thunder, the electrical energy, which explodes as lightning. It is virile or yang energy.

- The cow is the symbol for Earth, the Receptive, whose nature is submissive.

- The cockerel whose voice travels far into the night

represents the Gently penetrating energy of Wind.

- Thunder, as we have said is represented by the virile energy of the dragon.

- The pig is also an energetic creature, therefore yang and so shares in the virile nature. Also the pig is perceived as a lowly creature living in watery areas.

- Mountain stands as a guard on the treasures within, and so is symbolised by the dog.

- Fire is symbolised by the phoenix, which rises like the spirit from the ashes.

- The lake is represented the youngest daughter, whose nature is perceived as weak in an obstinate way, and so is symbolised by the goat.

One or two of the above examples may seem to be stretching the imagination somewhat, but I make use of them only to illustrate that their choice in the I Ching is not as arbitrary as they might appear. The primary use of such symbolism is to demonstrate that things having a yin nature must follow the principles of that nature. Therefore the earth, female and priest in following their yin nature, are yielding. We might say that this satisfies the principles of their earth-ness, female-ness and priest-ness. The same applies to heaven, man and sage as they follow the direction assigned to them by the virile nature of yang, they satisfy the principles of their man-ness, heaven-ness and sage-ness.

Nuclear Trigrams

The nuclear trigrams are represented in the following manner.

The lower nuclear trigram is made up of second third and fourth lines, while the upper nuclear trigram consists of the third fourth and fifth lines.

An example would look like this:

```
1 ———————
2 ———————        ] Upper nuclear trigram
3 ——  ——    ]  ]
4 ———————   ]  ]
5 ———————   ] Lower nuclear trigram
6 ——  ——
```

CONSULTING THE ORACLE

There are various procedures used to consult the I Ching, some of which are traditional i.e., the use of yarrow stalks and Chinese coins, but for this introductory volume we can use three English two pence coins. These coins serve our purpose because simply because they have a two on the tail side, and if we assign a three to the reverse side we can begin our consultation.

Before making our approach we need to formulate the question, keeping in mind the words of the sage, '*If we ask small questions we receive small answers and achieve small changes. Asking large questions stimulates character growth.*' Remember that the book was written by sage-kings to help those who wished to follow in their footsteps, and become men of character. Formulate your enquiry and throw the coins.

The method requires six throws of the coins, and builds a tower of yin and yang lines from the bottom up. Tails are worth two, heads three, giving us four possible results.

- Three heads is a total of nine, and represents yang. This is a changing line.

- Three tails totals six, representing yin and is also a changing line.

- Two tails and one head totalling seven is also yang, but unchanging.

- One tail, two heads comes to eight and represents yin, also unchanging.

Building our tower, remembering to start at the bottom, we might end up with a sequence like this:

First throw = seven, second = six, third = seven, fourth = eight, fifth = nine   sixth = eight.

Our structure looks like this:

```
8  — —
9  ———
10 — —
11 ———
12 — —
13 ———
```

To identify the hexagram, use the key. The lower trigram (bottom three lines) is to be found down the left side of the page; the upper trigram (top three lines) is across the top.

Our hexagram is number 63 After Completion. We now read the text and the appropriate lines. Only those lines described as changing lines (sixes and nines) concern us. When we have spent some time in quiet contemplation, of the meaning of the hexagram, and its application to our question, we can then construct the final part of the oracle's reply. As we have changing lines in the second and fifth places, we build our new hexagram as if those changes have been made. This implies that we have accomplished the transformation demanded by the time, thereby altering our condition. The hexagram would now read as follows:

```
8  ___  ___
6  ___  ___
8  ___  ___
7  _____
9  _____
7  _____
```

Our new hexagram is number 11 Peace, of which we read only the text, describing the situation after transformation.

If there are no changing lines, no sixes and nines, then all lines are to be consulted.

An important point concerning the reading is implicit in the central ideas of movement and rest. When we are able to rest we should meditate on the judgements of the hexagrams, thereby achieving change through wisdom. If our situation requires much activity, throwing the coins and active contemplation, i.e. objective awareness will help us attain the new perspective.

Summary

Formulate the question and throw the coins six times. Add the values of the coins as they fall- build the structure from the bottom. Refer to the key for the hexagram and read the text. If there are changing lines read these only, if there are none, all lines apply. Use the changing lines to construct the final hexagram, and read only the text.

Meditation and active contemplation should be employed to gain a different perspective.

1   Ch'ien – The Creative

Heaven over heaven
Fourth month May–June
All lines are strong and bright.

The nature of heaven is strong spiritual movement, and is personified throughout this hexagram. It brings light in all forms, to all levels of experience, expressed through the work of God and His servants, the sage-kings. Because the trigrams are repeated, they denote endurance of the qualities required by the ruler in the fifth place. These attributes are faith, strength, tolerance and integrity.

Judgement

The movement of the creative is expressed in four terms. From sublimity comes the primal cause, the idea; success describes how the idea then expresses itself by taking conscious form; furthering describes how it then moves beings to their proper nature, and perseverance is the manner in which this proper relation is maintained. The sage-king recognises the need for character development, through six stages, epitomised by the lines. Each of these changes comes in its time and requires spirit and patience. This is how the first two of the terms 'sublime success' is expressed in the world of men. The result of this process is that the superior man finds and follows his true nature, which in turn is to aid others in following the same path. This action is called 'furthering

through perseverance'. The man of character is said to
'Mount toward heaven on six dragons, then the clouds
pass and rain falls everywhere'. This means that his
character expands through the continuous
relationship of the lines, and spiritual sustenance,
symbolised by rain, is dispensed to all.

Image

Creative energy repeated is the image of continuous
movement within time. The idea that comes from this
is character growth, or persistent inner expansion.
The superior man removes all that is defective form
himself, so that his true nature can shine forth.

The lines
First line

The lowest line is the same as that of thunder, where
the spiritual force is still unseen. Here the character of
the sage has, as yet, not been unveiled. He is still
without work, but all that is required is patience,
because such energy is not given without purpose.

Second line

The character of this line works with others to
improve their lot and has a direct connection with the
central character in the fifth place. This connection
can be seen as external that is with a spiritual guide or
as internal with his spiritual centre.

Third line

The third line quite often suffers through extreme
reactions, but the creative character is so strong that
he learns from all of his excesses. As he creates a great

fellowship about himself, he recognises the dangers of ambition and pride and avoids them.

Fourth line

There is a choice for the line of the minister: to practice deeper meditation and acquire the expansion of the sage-king or to work directly with people and grow in this way. There is no judgement either way, for each must find and follow his true nature.

Fifth line

The central character has reached the peak of growth and his fame spreads. All who reach out to him receive benefit through finding their own inner strengths.

Sixth line

The top line signifies the arrogance that comes from isolation. This character believes himself to be superior to others, requiring help from no one. Such an attitude accrues from an incorrect use of the instructions as laid out in the steps below, and represents obstructed growth.

2 K'un – The Receptive

Earth over earth
Receptivity is yielding
Tenth month November–December
Winter solstice

The receptive power resides in the conscious world, that of the senses, spacial rather than temporal. It represents the female power in contrast to the male energy of the creative. The yin power is activated by the yang, to which it has an attitude of yielding, a disposition reflected in other relationships such as son to father, minister to prince. The second line is the ruler, representing the nature of the world and the follower, which is lowly, in comparison to that of heaven, whose place is the fifth line and whose nature is to lead. This relationship, of submitting to a higher power, is in the nature of things. It is only when the yin power attempts to lead that an unnatural condition occurs. From this condition comes evil and disease.

Judgement

The judgement expresses the nature of the receptive and the laws by which it must abide. As with the first hexagram we have the linked attributes of 'sublime success, furthering through perseverance…' In this case however the words '…of a mare.' are added. The mare is used as the symbol for earth because it of its tireless energy as it roams across the vastness of land,

and so furthers though perseverance. The receptive captures the heavenly seed giving form to this life force and conforming perfectly to the creative, achieving sublime success. The superior man is perceived as acquiescent to those forces, which guide him through the uncharted difficulties of life, so that he can conform to his nature by following the intuitions he receives.

Image
The repetition of the trigrams symbolises the vastness of the world and the perfection of its nature, in giving birth to all things originated by the power of heaven. The superior man broadens the scope of his character by enduring his earthly condition, and accepting direction from the voice of the creative within. In this way the vast depth and weight of worldly troubles does not affect him.

The lines   *First line*

The first line describes the natural order of danger: 'Hoarfrost is always followed by ice'. If we are aware of the implications of our actions before they assume overwhelming proportions, we can halt their effects in time. Imagining that denying small defects does not eventually lead to greater evils is a delusion. The one follows the other as certainly as solid ice follows frost.

                                              Second line

The ruling line depicts the primary attributes of the receptive power: adapting to the laws of heaven, it gives all living things their nature. The superior man has a constant enthusiasm for the work that leads to perfection of character, and by following the intuitive process, invariably finds the right course.

Third line

Vanity is a defect of the man of instincts, but the superior man rejects fame in favour of humility. From such a position his character becomes strong and he is able to make changes anonymously, changes that bear fruit for which others can be credited. This line describes the duty of the superior man as setting things in motion to be completed by others.

Fourth line

The mediating line has no correspondence with the ruler and therefore must withdraw into seclusion. This isolation is the correct action to take in these circumstances, because it would be vulnerable to misinterpretation if it ventured forward on its own strength. The fourth line defines the attitude of the receptive when resting, as cautious.

Fifth line

Self-restraint is the primary asset of the superior man as he seeks to infuse others with enthusiasm, and so to initiate positive changes in their lives. No recognition is required, for the outcome depends on the willingness and effort of the other.

Sixth line

In the tenth month of the Chinese calendar the sun is at its lowest point and the dark power seeks to rule the world. Its control is momentary however, for the solstice takes place and the sun again begins its ascent to power. The sixth line represents the egoistic attitude of the man who aspires to godhood, and the inner battle that ensues from such arrogance.

3 Chun – Difficulty at the beginning
Water over thunder

The first and fifth are yang lines and rule the hexagram. The bottom line represents the force of Thunder still underground. This is the first son the appointed voice of heaven, who is designated by the central line in the fifth place. The hexagram as a whole depicts the difficulty of his birth. When the two primary powers first unite, it is like the chaos of energies prior to a thunderstorm: water, representing spiritual energy is above, and Thunder as the Word of God is below. It is only when both find their proper station that balance is achieved and pressure is removed, just as tension in the air is cleared after the storm.

Judgement
The trigram of water also represents danger. The danger in a new beginning comes from not knowing the proper action to take, so one is required to seek guidance from others who know the correct path. When everything is in confusion and it looks like one could be overcome, energetic action is needed. The I Ching calls this action 'supreme success, furthering through perseverance'. The superior man in his first awakenings requires a strong fellowship about him, for direction and support.

Image

Thunder must pass through water, i.e. danger, in order to find its proper place. The time before this birth is full of confusion and danger, but within chaos are to be found the patterns for order. After the birth, when the energies have found their place, we have a new beginning.

The lines	*First line*

This line is the one of the rulers, but it can only do so through a humble attitude. Keeping sight of the goal and persevering through the initial difficulties ensures a successful outcome.

Second line

The time is not right for this line to take positive action, though the strong personality below offers help. If this help is accepted, it must be unconditional, because the allegiance of this line is to the central character in the fifth place. If we wait for the proper time, the changes we require for growth will come of their own accord.

Third line

Here the instinctive reactions to danger are to force our will and battle our way out. This would only increase the danger. The correct response is to seek guidance and wait for the proper time to act.

Fourth line

The fourth line has the insight to wait until his assistance is called for, rather than blindly pressing forward, but when the opportunity arises it must act energetically or the moment will pass.

Fifth line

This is the second ruling line, being a strong line in the correct place, but its work cannot be fulfilled because of the confusion of the overall situation. Recognising and accepting the great difficulties of the time means that the central character can continue to make small changes, until the state of confusion is relieved.

Sixth line

This personality isolates himself, then falls into a condition of self-pity. If he makes the required effort and reaches out for help with humility, the whole of his situation will change for the better.

4   Meng – Youthful Folly
Mountain over water

The second and fifth line rule. The second strong line
teaches and directs through the fifth line, which is a
willing helper and in accord with its work. The fresh
spring that bubbles from the foot of the mountain,
flows this way and that over the ground. This
represents the vital energy of youth rushing carelessly
here and there. The water has not yet cut a pathway
for itself, just as youth has not learned to limit its
energies. Time, experience and proper guidance help
to resolve the difficulties of ignorance and over
exuberance.

Judgement
The rashness of youth is a natural state, and the
hexagram of youthful folly depicts the correct manner
in which this condition can be altered. Everything
depends on an honest acceptance of the present
situation, and a willing and open-minded attitude
toward the new teaching. The teacher like the oracle
ought to give clear and simple instruction, ignoring
wasteful questioning while rewarding good work. The
second line is the primary ruler of the hexagram,
representing the old sage teaching the young sage in
the fifth place, the second ruling line.

Image

The spring bursts energetically from the base of the mountain, seeking out places to fill up, then moving on. The energy of youth works in the same way, pushing experiences to the limit, then moving on without satiety. In this way youth is open to new ideas, and requires a good teacher in order that the energy is channelled correctly.

The lines   *First line*

Childhood is a time of play, but eventually this must end and a more serious attitude should be cultivated. This is the time to teach the basic laws, of nature and society.

Second line

This is the place of the teacher whose attitude needs to be tolerant and forgiving. If he is open-minded and clear in his instruction, he will have good students, if not they will respond in like manner and he will receive no respect. If he is to be the leader of a group or society of people, then he must treat them all impartially.

Third line

A personality ruled by instincts is self-centred to the extreme. Seeking to further himself by an ingratiating attitude, he continuously misses the mark. If the teacher ignores such obvious overtures, then the student may eventually seek him out in a more humble manner.

Fourth line

The man fated to stand on the bridge, between the world of the spirit and the world of the senses, must himself be clear in his thoughts and attitudes. If he receives no guidance in his youth, it is likely he will be overwhelmed by illusion and fantasy, and his life will be a succession of humiliating circumstances. His only hope is that he will find a fellowship able to redirect him to his original purpose.

Fifth line

Though this line is weak, it has a direct correspondence with the sage in the second place, who accepts him as a student. His openness is like that of a child, and so he is able to learn with humility and trust.

Sixth line

This line represents a situation in which a personality, like that of the third line, persistently presses forward, hoping to gain an advantage not due to him. If the rejection and penalty are also instinctive, then the student will learn nothing, if they are too mild then the fool becomes more foolish. A wise teacher remains objective, so that the student can become aware of his excessive behaviour and learn how to limit himself.

51

5 Hsu – Waiting (Nourishment)
Water over heaven

Water is perceived as the basic requirement for man, and the idea of rainclouds in the sky represents a condition of patiently waiting. In the same way that rain provides sustenance for the maintenance and growth of the community, spiritual energy provides the key for its moral expansion, and so the image of waiting is clear. The idea of patience comes from knowing that nature, not man decides when rain should fall, and that destiny depends on the Divine will. The attribute of water is danger, while that of heaven is perseverance, which suggests that dangers are overcome by faith in the end result.

Judgement
This hexagram represents a time when the weaknesses within the character are exposed, and when our eventual fate depends entirely on how we deal with danger that approaches from within and without. Faith is the moment to moment certainty of success, overcoming all fears and emotional reactions to the contrary, which comes when we are willing to totally accept the truth of our situation. The character cannot grow in a delusion.

Image

The image of waiting for destiny might seem to suggest a period of inactivity, but this would be entirely erroneous, for we are waiting for only one aspect of our situation to fulfil itself. In the meantime we are occupied in strengthening ourselves and our community for the struggle ahead. The lines represent the responses of the strong character as the threat approaches.

The lines	*First line*

When the danger is still at a distance we have a feeling of restlessness. It is necessary that we recognise this sense for what it is, an awakening of the intuitive processes. This quiets the inner disturbance, which might cause us to rush about aimlessly trying to remove the uneasiness. Waiting, for this line, means the simple performance of duty until the time for defensive action arrives.

Second line

The threat is nearer, as indicated by the nature of the upper trigram, and the disturbance manifests as irritability and gossip. Again, the solution lies in recognising the nature of the anxiety as an indication of spiritual awareness. This prevents a decline into negative thinking.

Third line

Now the danger is so close that we go out to meet it driven by aggressive instincts. We manage to pull back in time, sensing the seriousness of our position.

Waiting includes a withdrawal of forces until such time as we can perceive the true nature of the threat.

Fourth line

The danger is all around us waiting for the first sign of weakness, but this is a yin line, and therefore capable of restraint. This suggests that the best way to overcome evil is not to confront it directly.

Fifth line

The central character of this hexagram has achieved enlightenment, and recognises that the greatest enemy to evil is happiness. His teaching is that the joy of living is the solution to all spiritual disease.

Sixth line

This is the high point of danger and we are at the jumping off place. At the moment of defeat, however, help comes from an unforeseen quarter, the three bottom lines. Because of their lowly place we might be moved to ignore their strength, but this is not the time for stubborn prejudice, rather an open-mindedness born of an honest recognition of our position.

6 Sung – Conflict

Heaven over water
Where there is conflict, there is no love

Heaven rises and the waters descend, the image of separation and conflict. Great endeavours require a singularity of purpose, whereas this hexagram shows contrasting natures, therefore the action counselled is for careful preparation.

The upper trigram presses up into the light, with determination, while the lower slides insidiously, into the black abyss. Each follows its nature, and so conflict occurs.

Judgement

If the hostility is to be neutralised, then one of the parties must negotiate terms. This falls to the superior man, because only he can act without bias. This is not a compromise, only a willingness to accept the other point of view, without complying with it. A strong, crafty personality seeks to drag others down to his level. He does this by attempting to excite them into overstepping the mark, so that they fall into the hidden abyss. The solution is to make no decisions based on unclear judgements, and prepare a strategy, which includes knowledge of the opponent's plan of attack. If ones preparations are complete, then the enemy is defeated before he begins. This is called 'meeting the enemy half-way'.

Image

The trigrams naturally oppose each other; therefore we have the image of conflict. If one knows the nature of the enemy and one's self, the conflict is neutralised. Action does not mean individual acts

The lines   First line

In the opening moves of a conflict, before the emotions are involved, it is possible to withdraw with grace. This then is the best action.

                                                        Second line

The solution for this line is to disguise its nature and withdraw into the background. Such a strategy is necessary when in the enemy territory.

                                                        Third line

The danger for this line is that it occupies the place of the instincts, and is restless for battle. No conflict will occur if it realises that the threat is empty, that its nature cannot be taken from it.

                                                        Fourth line

The place of the mediator, but this line at first desires conflict. Such is the cunning nature of the threat, that even priests are tempted to take part. It hears the words of the strong character in the line above and withdraws from the struggle.

                                                        Fifth line

The attributes of this line are those of a leader great character. He enters the field of battle, and is able to avert disaster by his superior strategy.

Sixth line

The top line typifies a personality who is unable to retreat. His strength is great enough to give him a resounding victory, but in the end the enemy wins, for he is attacked endlessly and knows no peace.

7   Shih – The Army

Earth over water

When threatened, individuals crowd together.

Water within the earth symbolises the energy resources within people. In times of peace each performs his individual task, but when war threatens they become a unit or body. The trigrams signify danger within and obedience without, descriptive of the qualities necessary for an army to be an effective force. The rulers of the hexagram are the second and fifth lines. Of these the fifth line represents the prince, who commissions the second line as his commander.

This suggests disciplining ones character in order that, when threatened, one behaves in a correct and justified manner.

Judgement

The energies of the people must be redirected if they are to perform as a single unit. This requires a personality able to secure the confidence of the people by his integrity: one who can stand alongside them at the centre of things and inspire them with enthusiasm. Such a leader ought to be an accomplished strategist in order to direct their energies under fire in the most competent manner. An excellent strategy is one, which includes as little hostility as possible: one in which the preservation of life is paramount. This must be extended to the defeated in retreat. There is no dignity in the annihilation of a vanquished enemy. This should also apply to defects ousted from ones character.

Image
Secure within the earth, water flows quietly: an image of the hidden energy of the people in peacetime. The primary aim of a ruler ought to be to preserve the resources of the people. To do this means employing a competent government, and an astute commander for the armed forces. This applies equally in the sense of self-development, where the energies and attributes of ones person ought to be disciplined by the character.

The lines   *First line*

When the army is set to enter into battle for the first time, it must do so as a disciplined unit. If the justification for conflict is clear to all, they will enter the battle with enthusiasm.

Second line

Troops will fight with vigour when their superiors share in their difficulties. For the commander to enter into battle with them suggests he is assured of victory, and when this victory comes he receives honours from the ruler.

Third line

This line is in a state of agitation, as with a person directed by instincts. They all rise up at once and try to take control, resulting in confusion and demoralisation. An army without a leader is undisciplined, and therefore in danger of being overcome by superior forces.

Fourth line

The forces do not have the energy to deal with the opponent. It is wise to make a strategic withdrawal, until ones resources are once again equal to the task.

Fifth line

The enemy has entered the field of combat and the commander has made the decision for battle. He does this, knowing he has the support of his superior, and the control of his forces. His strategy is based on experience and skill, and prepared well in advance of the opponent's actions. His instructions are fair and humane, and unlike the example of the third line, are not based on unprincipled motives. Follow this example carefully.

Sixth line

All those involved in the victory should be honoured, but in different ways, and according to their nature. Therefore, those who fought gallantly ought to be trusted with property and responsible position: those who fought for personal gain should be paid in money. The suggestion regarding character growth is that, even though defects can sometimes aid in survival, one ought not to be deluded into giving them a place of power.

8   Pi – Holding Together
Water over earth
Unity

The fifth line draws the five weak lines together by his strength of character, and all benefit from the unity of interests. The waters of the earth continuously separate and return to a unified form, as oceans, rivers and seas. This symbolises the spiritual nature, which unites all things together.

Judgement
Unity is the core of fellowship, and this centre requires a strong character in order that the union is persevering. If we have a desire to take on the work, we should enquire of the oracle if we have these attributes, because if it is only wish-fulfilment then we will create chaos rather than order. On the other hand if we recognise the need to be a central character, and do not have the desire for the work, then we should find another fellowship.

Image
Water constantly flows over the world, giving life to all things equally. In the same way, any society should be unified through the agreement of all its members, in order that that society can behave as a single entity. This is the spiritual nature of any fellowship, when its basic aims are in accord with the primary

requirements of each and every member.

The lines *First line*

The desire for fellowship of the bottom line is simple and sincere, and because of this it draws attention to itself from the strong line above. Through such simple honesty great relationships are born.

Second line

The second line corresponds to the ruling line because their spiritual natures are in accord, but if this line should seek to gain an important position in society as a result, then it loses its relationship.

Third line

Care must be taken not to be drawn into relationships by our social instinct: relationships, which are not in harmony with the basic requirements of the fellowship to which we belong. This is not to say that we should have no other social arrangements, only that we ought not to be controlled by our instinctive natures.

Fourth line

The minister openly carries the message of the ruling character, dispensing hope and strength to the other members of the community. His relationship should remain firm and constant, so that he is not drawn away from the simple attitude of the man at the centre.

Fifth line

The man who chooses the central place does so because his character requires him to. His purpose is to lead others to know their strengths and that the simplest way of doing so is by sacrificing their weaknesses. Not everyone cares to make such a sacrifice, and those who do may not be able to make the transition immediately, but if he is patient and waits for the correct time they will approach him eventually. In this way a fellowship of like-minded individuals is formed.

Sixth line

This line is unable to find the will to approach the strong line, and so remains outside of fellowship and alone.

9 Hsiao Ch'u – Taming of the small
Wind over heaven
The nature of character
Character is refined by attending to small things

The fifth line is the ruling line and as a part of the trigram of wind, holds together in a gentle manner with the fourth line, which is weak. Through this example, all of the other yang lines permit the yin line, in the place of the minister to restrain them in their forward movement. This aids in the growth of character, in that the strong lines of the Creative, the father, submit to the gentle influence of the eldest daughter, to deal with immediate difficulties.

Judgement
The hexagram reflects a time when great achievements are not possible. There are obstacles, which though minor, need to be dealt with before continuing on ones course. This, because they will grow into major problems if ignored at this stage. The situation does not demand forceful measures, however, since the difficulties can be checked by gentle inducement toward the good. A simple attitude and a flexible resolve are the faculties required.

Image
The wind travels everywhere, but its influence is immediate, whereas the energy of the creative is at the centre of man's character, where it produces long-

term effects. For the lower power to influence the greater requires that they be related in trust. The father and oldest daughter have such a relationship, and it is through her influence and gentle approach that the tyrant of self-will is held in check.

The lines   *First line*

The augury for this line is favourable, in that on encountering the obstacle of the fourth line, it obeys the will of the ruling line and withdraws to its place. This designates a character with both wisdom and tolerance.

Second line

This line is at the centre of the creative trigram and therefore strong in character. It follows the example of other members of its fellowship, and returns to its place to await further commands from the ruling line.

Third line

This line tends to drive forward instinctively, using its own strength. This is its nature and so there is no great blame, and anyway the fourth line is not as weak as it seems, and so stands up to it. As always, when instinct and self-will are combined there is conflict, for others have instincts also. This personality is driven back to its place, suffering a blow to its pride. This can be profitable if he is willing to take the rejection in his stride, for only then can it be seen that this is one of the small modifications advised by the fourth line.

Fourth line

The courage of this line is apparent. A gentle power succeeds in restraining stronger and more wilful energies, in order to accomplish something of benefit to all. The leader in the fifth place, who endorses its efforts, knows the sincerity of this line.

Fifth line

The nature of loyalty is demonstrated by the relationship between the fifth and fourth lines, which in this line is trustworthiness and in the yin line devotion. The complementary powers of yin and yang behave as their true natures dictate when they work together, and all within their field of activity benefit accordingly.

Sixth line

The work has produced a successful outcome. The gentle force, having made this possible by directing the necessary changes, must now step down. There is a danger that the top line will succumb to the danger of the third line, which is that of egoistic delusion, but if it takes the opportunity to rest all goes well.

10 Lu – Treading

Heaven over lake
Conduct means walking the walk
Treading is the foundation of character

Joy is having determination, which manifests in a
gentle demeanour. Growth of character is founded on
the idea of walking the walk, which means adhering
to the fundamentals of right conduct. To be strong in
ones resolve, while being influenced by an open heart,
results in the kind of behaviour that has great
influence. This is the hexagram of Treading, from
which we can learn the simple forms required for
right action.

Judgement

Joy, is the subtlest of those internal energies which
direct us in a positive manner. The Creative on the
other hand, is direct and overwhelming. For the first
to influence the second in its direction there must be
an unconditional relationship between the two. A
relationship based on complete trust. The hexagram
depicts this connection as between father and
youngest daughter, where the parent allows the child
to alter the manner of his dealings with people, by the
example of her cheerful approach. One can also see
here how the more powerful energies of ones
personality are controlled, or redirected, by pleasanter
feelings.

Image

Each follows its nature. The unswerving directive of the sage-king is highest, and therefore leads, but the nature of joy is to make ones unselfish actions pleasant. In terms of social behaviour and position, this hexagram suggests that, those with a broader viewpoint lead those whose skill is to infect others with joy in their work. In the formation of character, reason and feelings form a hierarchy in which reason must lead, but allow itself to be positively influenced by feelings.

The lines   *First line*

In this line we come to understand the merits of correct motivation. Achieving progress through the instincts results in arrogance once one has succeeded in ones ambitions. This is unavoidable because the instincts, by their nature, are self-serving, but if the motivation for progress is to achieve something of benefit to all, this must result from the simplest of actions.

Simple actions means to follow ones true nature, alone if necessary.

Second line

The strength of character of this line is expressed as that of the sage-king who requires nothing from the world except to follow his nature. This is possible because the line is central and the duty clear. As with the first line, he is happy to walk the road alone, and work anonymously.

Third line

Here, there is no clear direction or duty and one does not have the strength to compete with greater forces, such as those of the instincts. This conduct can only be viewed as correct when in the service of higher ideals.

Fourth line

In this line, one again is depicted as battling with strong forces, but this line has both strength and a superior strategy and so succeeds in its resolve.

Fifth line

This line is the ruler of the hexagram, in the place of the most power.

It has a duty to behave with energy and overcome without quarter. Success comes to it because it personifies the great leader, whose strategy has taught him to persevere in the direction of what is right. He succeeds because he 'Knows the enemy and knows himself'.

Sixth line

This line has nowhere to walk and can only justify past actions by their results. If the inventory shows a good outcome, one can be sure of ones motivations. If the opposite is true, then it is necessary to alter ones motivations by a change of direction i.e. toward Good.

11 T'ai – Peace
Earth over Heaven
February–March first month
Serenity

The energies of the earth move downward while those of heaven rise. In this hexagram, therefore, yin and yang are seen to meet and combine their influences, in order to unify the nature of things. The second and fifth lines govern the hexagram. They have become one force in order that the cycle of Nature can begin again in a new spring.

Judgement
Here, all conflicts have been removed. The channel of energy is unobstructed and peace prevails. In the outside world the forces of Nature are awakened and new life has begun to take form. In society, all that is correct is in the central position and there is a unity of interests and in general terms. Selfish motives have been put aside in favour of the greater good. Finally, as regards individual growth, the spirit directs the instinctual drives, and one can move toward further understanding and expansion.

Image
The channel for productive forces is freed of the substance of decay. In Nature this is a part of the cycle of the seasons, but in human terms has been brought about only by consistent effort toward the Good.

Mankind aids Nature by removing the blockages to new growth, thereby improving the harvest. For the superior man, it denotes a character unencumbered by destructive defects. By persistently recognising and removing those things, which are inconsistent with the requirements of the time, his duties are clear to him.

The lines   *First line*

Because ones duties are clear, the desire to create a fellowship is primary. In this way like-minded people are attracted to each other, in order to accomplish that which they could not do of themselves.

Second line

This is a strong line in a weak place, being of the lower trigram, and therefore requires the help of the six in the fifth in order to provide the gentle outlook required. This is necessary because, in forming fellowships, many will not have achieved the removal of their more destructive elements, and only a gentle and understanding attitude can gain their confidence. One ought to be willing to go to any lengths to accomplish such an open approach.

Third line

This yang line seeks to project its energy outwards, being rich in vitality. A setback at this time might generate despondency, but if one remembers that evil is never destroyed, only arrested, then one does not become complacent. With this knowledge, the determination of this line can remain stronger than the vicissitudes of life.

Fourth line

Even though this line is in the place of the minister, it is able to come together with those personified in line two without preaching, in the knowledge that those drawn together by inner conviction are equal in spirit.

Fifth line

The humility of this line is that it is willing to join with the yang line in the second place and treat it as equal. It is through the unity of their energies that new and productive associations are formed.

Sixth line

This line corresponds with the third and suffers through its over-exuberance. Danger comes to it as a result, but if it retires into its fellowship all will be well. The only danger lies in challenging evil alone. This would be the most arrogant of mistakes.

12 P'i – Standstill

Heaven over Earth
August–September seventh month
Second and fifth lines rule

Although the structure of the hexagram appears to be
in harmony, i.e. heaven above the earth, the opposite
is true. The light is moving away, while the earth falls
into darkness. In terms of nature and the seasons this
is a natural condition, it is the beginning of autumn
and there is a natural decline into darkness. In terms
of human affairs, however, the decay is due to
character defects. Darkness is within and the light
cannot enter, therefore the creative power must
continue to withdraw until the time of Return.

Judgement
It is a time in which darkness approaches and those
who shun the light follow in its wake. The only
recourse is to withdraw into solitude until the proper
time. Intellectualism and emotionalism are dangerous
temptations and should be avoided at all costs: to give
in to their seduction would only increase the
obstruction.

Image
There are those that have observed ones actions from
the shadows, who consider that everything has a
price. They feel it right to offer position and fame in
exchange for what they believe to be skills. Their

motives, however, are for personal gain, and this would eventually mean the corruption ones principles. Therefore it would be futile to be tempted by what they have to offer. To fall beneath their temptations would be like kneeling before a false spirit.

The lines   First line

The first three lines are all yin, and therefore weak lines. However, they can be strengthened if they work together, toward the Good, represented by the fifth line. This line exemplifies the idea of withdrawing from danger in these dark times.

Second line

Those who are depicted in the Image have begun their attempts to persuade and flatter. Though others may benefit in small ways if their offers are accepted, the overall gain would be nil, and ones principles would have been lost in the process. For this line, success comes from a quiet withdrawal.

Third line

Here shame is the key to success. Self-will has created an illusion of strength in the mind, but the heart rejects this ploy and feels shame. This indicates a change toward the Good.

Fourth line

This line is the place of the mediator, and if we feel called to undertake the work involved, we must be sure that the call comes from the Good (the fifth place) and not the place of self will (the six in the third place). If we are sure, then those who are influenced in a similar way will be attracted, and a fellowship will be formed.

Fifth line

This ruling line represents the superior power and place. Here the leader has begun to restore balance, but is aware of the dangers of cultivating self-satisfaction. In these times there comes a general feeling of liberation. The darkness is overcome and everyone rejoices, but this is the time when the leader watches the shadows, for danger never rests. It too withdraws and works for a better moment.

Sixth line

In terms of the seasons, decay comes naturally and in its time. In autumn those things, which have soaked up the light of summer and have fulfilled their purpose, go through a natural process of decay. This process continues into regeneration. In human affairs, conscious effort is necessary if the situation is not to deteriorate into total ruin. The danger here is complacency.

13 T'ung jen – Fellowship with men
Heaven over flame

The yin line in the second place reaches up with humility to the central character in the fifth, and clings to the other lines in fellowship. A society of this type has a clear purpose and a strong character at its centre. The essence of fellowship is that, each of its members is willing to sacrifice the personal will for the good of the society as a whole. In this way the fellowship behaves as a single entity directed by the central will.

Judgement
Fellowships are not based on the will of cliques and factions: rather they reflect the composite will of all of humanity, answering its spiritual needs rather than its instinctive desires, fulfilling the requirements of the time. At the centre of such fellowships we find a superior personality, serving the community directly, and another to whom falls the central purpose of relaying the will of heaven.

Image
Flame reaches up to the fires of heaven for identification and fellowship, where the stars and their courses endure. Their movements represent the natural laws on which a free society must be based, so

that it too can endure. Though each member finds his own nature through the work of such communities, all accept that there must be some form of order for the fellowship to function as an efficient unit.

The lines	*First line*

When fellowships are in their infancy, or when its individual members first find unity, there is a great sense of oneness as each finds acceptance for himself and of others. If this humility is lost and special claims are made for some of its members, conflict results.

Second line

A fellowship ought to be open to all that wish to join, but if out of fear or pride the society becomes exclusive, or breaks up into power driven factions, it must eventually collapse for it can no longer follow the central will.

Third line

When men of instincts joins a fellowship they are unable to become one amongst many. They feel threatened by the idea of personal sacrifice, and so their fears cling to them and isolate them from the rest. Driven to blame others for their difficulties, they are eventually unable to be honest even with themselves, and either leave or hang around the fringes of the fellowship.

Fourth line

Strong personalities find fellowship difficult at first

because it is in their nature to lead or bend others to their will. This line represents such a man, who having entered a fellowship, attempts to seize control, but finds his efforts blocked at every turn. When his aggressive energy wanes he throws up his hands and enters in the correct manner.

Fifth line

The nature of fellowship itself is depicted through the relationship between this line and the second line. Both are separated in the first instance by the difficulties of the lines in between, but because it is in their destiny to combine, through perseverance and adherence to their correct natures all obstructions are removed, and they become one.

Sixth line

This line represents those societies whose relationships are based on a form of exclusivity, rather than as a benefit to all of mankind. They are not seen as at fault, for such a completely open fellowship is perceived as the ideal, but the suggestion is that working toward this ideal aids mankind's spiritual advancement.

14 Ta Yu – Possession in great measure

Flame over Heaven
Light shines evenly everywhere

The fifth line is the ruler and has humility. Those that
are humble are approachable, and so the strong lines
in the hexagram allow themselves to be lead. The
hexagram represents a time of strength and clarity,
when understanding increases and confusion retreats.
It is a time of great personal development.

Judgement
This is a time, where strength of character and clarity
of vision, are required for the work against evil to be
completed. Possessing the powers of heaven in
humility depends on a clear mind and firm
judgement. This judgement must be founded on the
knowledge of ones obligations and nature, which is
loyalty to truth.

Image
The sun shines on the good and the evil alike. It is
this, which furthers the truth, for it has no reason to
shun the light, whereas those things masquerading as
true, are exposed in their falseness. The light of the
humble character shines clearly and others are drawn
to it for aid. This is the way, or the nature, of Grace in
great measure. All lines give allegiance to the son of
heaven, in the fifth place.

The lines
First line

When we first experience such energy, we might disregard negative impulses from within and temptations from outside, but if we are aware that they exist, they have no power to thwart the Good that we can foster in others.

Second line

Here is the central point of the primary trigram, whose nature is duty, and there is a direct correspondence with the humble fifth line. Movement toward the Good, and in the midst of a strong fellowship, is indicated. There is much one can give to those who have little. Essentially, sharing is the key exercise of this hexagram- the sharing of spiritual energy.

Third line

This line is influenced by the instincts, but such is its humility in this case that it knows that its energy cannot be used selfishly, for it is clear that its power is not of the instincts. Knowing this, and that what it possesses is great, is both the mark of wisdom and the nature of sacrifice.

Fourth line

The clarity of insight of this, the minister, enables it to view the ruling line as the true leader. As priest, or mediator, he can pass on all that he receives and recognise the direction from which it comes. He carries the weight of responsibility as if it were no weight at all.

Fifth line

The energy of this line is direct and true, because it is central and in the upper trigram. It is a weak line but this works in its favour because it is in accord with the strong central line of the lower trigram. This correspondence creates a great humility that cannot be worn down by mere circumstance. It is this humble outlook that infuses the other lines.

Sixth line

Heaven places much responsibility on this line, imbuing it with the clarity and energy of the sage. The nature of the prophet is dedication, and he directs this devotion toward the line below. He recognises that the man depicted in the fifth line, is the son of heaven and encourages allegiance to him.

15 Ch'ien – Humility
Earth over mountain
Through humility one holds tightly to character

The third line rules as the only light line, but takes its place in the lower trigram below that of all of feminine lines. The mountain is the youngest son, depicted here as giving precedence to the mother. This symbolises humility.

Judgement
The arrogant are brought low and the humble raised up. This natural law of increase and decrease is expressed through the waxing and waning of sun and moon, the wearing down of hills and the building of mountains from valleys, and the deflation of ego in contrast to the expansion of character. Recognising that mankind rejects those who are arrogant and follow the humble, the superior man works anonymously to further the great cause.

Image
The mountain that was raised up is now covered by earth, but its wealth and qualities still exist. This is the image of humility, when greatness is invisible because it has raised others to its own heights. This is how the humble man works when he elevates others above himself.

The lines   *First line*

A humble man take on all kinds of difficulties
overcomes many obstructions, because success and
failure mean the same to him. People do not resist
him, because he makes no demands on them and
keeps his work simple.

Second line

The attributes of the second line are correctness and
humility, because it serves and supports the ruling
line above it.

Third line

The character of this line is strong yet humble and is
able to perform great tasks and make significant
changes in the world. This is because he doesn't look
at himself, only at the work, and others feel able to
approach him and offer their skills.

Fourth line

This line must translate the will of the fifth line and
carry it below to the ruling line. He must then inform
the people of the work involved, and see that all are
correctly employed. The position of mediator requires
a sense of responsibility and much humility, and
should not be taken lightly.

Fifth line

Sometimes the central character must remind people
of their responsibilities, in order that the work can be
completed. If this is done without aggression or
drama, then those involved will accept the
admonition with good grace and fulfil their
obligations.

Sixth line

When conflict forces positive action, it is a mistake to withdraw with the delusion that retreat equals humility. Hostility requires an immediate response, anything short of this implies cowardice rather than humility.

16 Yu – Enthusiasm

Thunder over Earth
The law of nature

Thunder, the eldest son, inspires the world i.e. the devoted to follow. This exhilarating movement is called enthusiasm, and denotes the presence of God as experienced in the world of man. The movements connote the laws within the nature of things. It is in the nature of mankind to experience fervour. The fourth line is the mediator and the ruler of the hexagram. It is a single line in the midst of broken lines and symbolises a door. The character depicted by this line is therefore a doorman or gate-man.

Judgement
The fourth line is the epitome of character, and has the power to enthuse those around it. This perfection of character is possible, only in someone who has given up worldly values (a yang line surrounded by yin lines), but who nevertheless is able to identify with the difficulties of those seeking to find inner worth. Through the action of natural law fellowships are formed, for what is in the deepest nature of man he follows with enthusiasm. Enthusiasm is the energy of God. Thunder, Chen, is the first son of heaven, the voice or Word of God.

Image

Drum and cymbal in ceremonies such as Chinese New Year represented thunder the voice of God. Thus was the prototype for music formed. As thunder moves the heart to veneration, so music moves the heart to open up to joy and enthusiastic movement. The idea of a doorman, who can induce this opening of the heart, is the central image of this hexagram. Pictured also is the idea that the inner temple can be reached through this simple movement.

The lines   *First line*

The first line corresponds to the fourth and brags of this. It calls attention to itself, as if it had energy of its own, and negative forces are drawn to it. Only the compassion of the strong fourth line can save this line from itself.

Second line

Central and strong, being a part of the nuclear trigram, mountain, it knows when to be still and when to move. In terms of the cultivation of character this line perceives the first movements of defects and acts with enthusiasm toward their correction. Withdrawing into the stillness at the centre, this line is able to apprehend the will of God and contemplate the next forward movement.

Third line

This line represents the kind of personality, which instinctively seeks to depend on those with greater strength, meaning that he expects them to act for him.

This is unwise for changes are initiated by our own actions. The patience of the strong personality in the line above might eventually lift this helpless one to its feet.

Fourth line

Surrounded by those who depend on ones enthusiastic support, some of whom will constantly take the wrong course before correcting themselves, while others create unhealthy dependencies, one could be overwhelmed by doubts. This line, however, is gifted with great enthusiasm, and such doubts serve only to create a compassion for those with less strength, and thus a great fellowship is formed.

Fifth line

In the heart of the upper trigram, a disease has entered, and endeavours to overcome the desire for Good. If there is a constant awareness, of the nature of this spiritual malady, then survival is likely. There is no enthusiasm for this line, but no despair either for it is directly connected with the line below, and shares in its strength.

Sixth line

This line feeds on enthusiasm as if it were a drug. This condition arises because the ego is so blinded that it believes it is the power, and therefore indestructible. When the truth comes to this line, as with the bottom line, only humiliation can alter its course toward a better philosophy of life.

17 Sui – Following

Lake over thunder
Winter – the image of resting
A leader, should know how to follow

The first and fifth lines, by standing beneath weak lines, show the humility necessary to promote a following. Thunder rests in the lake and prepares itself for a new movement in spring. Thunder is the eldest son who influences the youngest daughter to follow him, because he places her nature and needs above his.

Judgement

By his willingness to do this she perceives correctness in his character, and willingly follows his example. The criterion for a legitimate following is durability: without this, any group or fellowship will disintegrate at the first obstruction. This concept, where a following is created through adjusting to circumstances, rather than vice versa, is at the heart of every great society throughout history.

Image

The image is night and winter, a time for rest and recuperation of energies. Thunder, the voice of God, rests protected by the waters of the earth.

This suggests the preparation for a great birth, after which the protector will become the follower. The natural law of resting before action is exemplified here.

The lines

There is a change in the meaning of authority. The creative principal subordinates itself to the second line, in the place of the chosen. In this way the eldest son can learn what is required of him, in his immediate locality. When this is done, however, he must move out into the world wherever his duty takes him.

Second line

Here the second line, the female principle, is induced to let go of the small boy, in favour of the adult. Like the mother, this line must free the son to follow the will of the father.

Third line

In this, the line of the instincts and emotions, there is the danger of following fleeting desires, but also the recognition that there can be no character development in this way. The line above, a yang line draws him away from the second line, toward his destiny.

Fourth line

This yang line rests on two yin lines, which press upward and seek favours to which they are not entitled. If a dependency is created on such flattery, then the ego overcomes the desire to do the will of the father. Perseverance toward the good, is the solution to the self-will of the lower energies.

Fifth line

This is the ruler of the upper trigram whose attribute is joy. All who desire to follow their true nature must do so with enthusiasm and joy, each must and recognise the necessity for a primary objective. This line calls on the sage-king in the sixth place to come out of retirement and lead him.

Sixth line

The sage-king, having performed his duties and isolated himself from the world, must eventually return in order to aid the fifth line in following his nature.

18 Ku – Work on what has been spoiled
Mountain over wind/wood

Wind is gentle influence, which has no ineffectual against the immovable mountain. This means that all efforts become counter productive, as the will to continue decreases. This decrease develops into such a state of decay, that there appears to be no escape. The hexagram depicts a condition where the uncompromising will of the father, and the ineffectual will of the mother produce a spoiled outlook in their children. The character cannot evolve, because all efforts to remove the mountain of stale ideas, emotions and attitudes are futile. This is true, also, in society, when the archaic views of governments create sterility in the community. The result is despair. At the core of the hexagram, however, (the nuclear trigrams) Thunder rises from the Lake, and we can observe the chance of joyous movement toward positive change.

Judgement
Gentle movement cannot create the propulsion toward positive action, the problems are too great, and despair sets in. In the nuclear trigrams, where the voice of God combines with joyous energy, we find the potential for a different point of view, and the impetus required to overcome the dispirited

condition. This may not happen overnight, however, and a practical strategy, based on sound spiritual principles, is required if we are not to slip back into the old ways. The suggestion is to plan for three days, before we begin, and continue with determination for a further three days. In this way the I Ching demonstrates how end and beginning are intertwined.

Image

A mountain of old habits and an ineffectual will: the image of decay. When our strategy for living fails utterly, and becomes a barrier to growth, we arrive at a condition of despair. Having no place to go, we turn inwards and find the potential for a solution to all of our difficulties.

The lines   *First line*

The mind is filled with traditional solutions-productive in themselves, but when they allow for no creativity, they become a handicap. When we know the problem we have made the first move toward its solution, but blame is a negative trait by which the problem clings to us. This means we ought not to condemn the excessive discipline of the father.

Second line

Corresponding to the ruling line in the fifth place, the suggestion of this line is to be gentle and slow at the start. Again, there is the counsel against blame, this time of the mother.

Third line

Because of the willingness for reform, the over
enthusiasm of this line can be forgiven- even though
it causes some resentment. Be aware that blaming
others for our emotional condition creates a further
reaction in them, and we can end up with a battle of
instincts.

Fourth line

Here the problem has begun to manifest and take
control, and because of fear, a malaise sets in and no
effort is made to confront it. As this line is in the place
of the minister, it must allow faith to overcome the
fear to look within, and therefore find the energy to
endure.

Fifth line

The personality cannot create the new beginning on
its own- it must reach out to others to aid in the
recovery process. This line is central and therefore
correct in its desire for expansion, but also has the
humility to recognise its lack of energy and
understanding. It therefore seeks out fellowship with
others of like mind.

Sixth line

The top line depicts the sage who has already made
the long journey of self-discovery and who can
receive no more from society. This cannot be an
excuse for idleness, however, his work must continue
for the benefit of future generations.

19 Lin – Approach

Earth over lake
Becoming great
Twelfth month January–February

The idea of approach comes from the entrance of the two yang lines, the rulers, into the hexagram. This is viewed as the attribute of spiritual strength, about to disperse itself amongst the common people. The solstice has passed and the darkness retreats from the new light. Thus we have an image of a world preparing itself for the work of spring, so that its bounty will be great.

Judgement

The trigrams advance toward each other: the upper with love and the lower with joyousness. Further to this the new light offers strength to the approaching union, so that success is assured. The sage enters the world to direct and support any that require his help, but he must do so before the return of the dark months, and so he keeps his words simple and his actions easy so that nothing is wasted.

Image

The lake symbolises an inexhaustible supply of spiritual sustenance, surrounded by the earth, representing the community. They take what they need from the lakes, directing it to all areas of the land, just as the sage provides for the community through practical teaching. The nuclear trigrams are thunder below the earth, which also represents the return of the light power, prior to spring.

The lines	*First line*

The bottom lines move upward together, because they are of the same character, but this line presses against the line above in order to stimulate its first movement.

Second line

The humble character in the fifth place has called the first two lines and so they make their first approach. The character of this line is strong and his understanding of the time is clear. The work ahead needs to be done without question for what is involved follow a natural order, and time is limited.

Third line

The third line is an energetic place, but because this line is weak it tends to seek the easy work. This kind of attitude leads to complacency and a loss of impetus, but if there is remorse and a return to responsible work, humiliation vanishes.

Fourth line

The minister is an important person in society because his work involves contact with all persons in that community. Here he enlists the allegiance of the modest sage in the lowest place and treats him with the respect as an equal.

Fifth line

The yin line in the central place depicts a character of unusual insight and self-knowledge. He calls on those whose proficiency is established, and whose knowledge and understanding of the requirements of the time are greater than his, and allows them to do their work.

Sixth line

The top line stands in the place of the sage who has retired from public life and the concerns of the world, yet returns when his knowledge and expertise are in demand.

20 Kuan – Contemplation

Wind over earth
Eighth month September–October

In contemplation we observe the true nature of things- and the idea of wind gently penetrating into all things over the world, is a symbol of this. The rulers are the light lines at the top, which are not threatened as they observe the mass of dark lines approaching. Seeing clearly, superior men differentiate the good from the bad in people, and because they are not conditioned by the ego, can appeal to their true nature. The dark lines then follow their true disposition, and withdraw downwards.

Judgement

The nuclear trigrams of mountain and earth symbolise contemplation in that mountain also represents a temple, in this case the inner temple. During the act of deep meditation we enter the inner sanctum, and apprehend sacred truth. The sage translates what he learns at these times into practical demonstrations of God's laws, by openly differentiating between the real and the unreal, and through this others are influenced.

Image

The wind has an influence on everything it touches, as it blows over the world. Plants and animals are refreshed by its presence. In the same way, great leaders influence others by the simplicity of their expression and understanding.

The lines *First line*

Defiance is bound to strengthen ignorance and lead to ruin, but for some this appears to be a natural state, for which there can be no real blame. If someone is aware of the divine laws, and continues to disobey what he knows to be correct, only great shame comes to him.

Second line

The second line is usually correct in its view, but in this case it is like someone peeping through the letterbox, afraid to make contact with others. How can the work be done if we allow fear and introversion hold us back. It is necessary to find a teacher who can show us a different way.

Third line

This personality has learned to regulate his extremes by contemplating his defects, and moving toward their elimination. In this way he becomes more objective in his view and his work.

Fourth line

The strength of character of the minister is recognised by the teacher in the place above, who allows him to follow his own path. Independent action is possible if one has the willingness for the task at hand.

Fifth line

Having moved away from the illusion of self-satisfaction, the contemplation of the teacher and sage is a practical exercise, involving clear self-examination. If his influence on others bears fruit he can continue in the same vein, if not he alters his attitudes accordingly. This is the simple inventory of a man whose changes are in response to the effect he has on others.

Sixth line

The top line represents a sage who has transcended ego and instinct, whose contemplates the rise and fall of the powers of good and evil, in order that his teachings reflect the great demands of the time.

21 Shih ho – Biting through
Fire over thunder
Thunder and lightning

The trigrams of fire over thunder depict the energetic movement required to remove a dangerous obstacle. The nuclear trigrams of water and mountain provide the image for the immovable obstruction. The light force has accumulated at the centre of things, and can only be removed by explosive force.

Storms eliminate amassed energies, just as social rules eliminate the build up of criminal activity, which is naturally drawn to human culture. The construction of the lines depicts an open mouth, where the teeth and lips are unable to come together, due to an obstruction. The energies of the lines above and below must work together to remove the blockage.

Judgement
Harmony is essential, whether in society or individual, if there is to be a progressive movement. When this unity is blocked, the laws for the removal of the obstacle must be known to all. The fifth line is the ruler, and the lawgiver. He dispenses penalties, and so the criminal elements are dispersed, just as the tension in the atmosphere is dispersed after a storm.

Image
Thunder rises, and lightning explodes into the

atmosphere. Criminal laws ought to be this clear in their intent, and immediate in their execution. Obstructions to character growth should be dealt with in the same way. All of ones forces should be brought to bear on the defects involved, and so aid in their removal.

The lines	*First line*

The hindrance to forward movement, depicted in the lower line is simply stubbornness. The refusal to give up petty crime results in minor punishments, which is hopefully enough to make clear the necessity for an alteration in basic behaviour.

Second line

Here, the punishment seems to be excessive, due to its suddenness and energy content, but as the hexagram implies, these are the requirements to overcome criminal activities.

Third line

Penalties need to be administered in a just and clear manner, in order that all are aware of the outcome of breaking the laws. If punishments are meted out impulsively, as they were in those times before reason prevailed, criminals will react in a like manner. This is also true in character development, where endeavouring to remove one instinct by the use of another, only strengthens the barrier one is trying to remove.

Fourth line

The obstacles blocking progress are many and varied,

but their elimination is certain if one endures through the stresses of a difficult campaign. It is of primary importance that one is aware of the nature of all of the problems, however, if one is not to be lead into negative and disruptive conflicts.

Fifth line

This line is in the centre of justice and knows intuitively how to deal with situations. The picture of the superior man as following the laws of fate, and dispensing reward and punishment with, neither fear nor favour, illustrates a man who deals with others in the same manner as he deals with himself. Character growth depends on having a clear objective, and a willingness to behave in the manner demanded by the needs of the time.

Sixth line

The personality depicted is of an egoist, whose arrogance is so great he has become deaf to the quiet words from below. Even when the consequences of his corrupt actions finally overwhelm him, he is unable to blame himself.

22 Pi - Grace

Mountain over Fire
Contemplating form

In this hexagram the mountain is lit by fire. This comes from within the earth, not chaotically as from a volcano, but as a river of fire below the mountain. The mountain personifies stillness while fire is clarity, and so we see clearly that which is real. There is a harmony of movement within the structure for the flame reaches up, as does the nuclear trigram of thunder, while the lower nuclear trigram of water has a downward movement. The mountain too presses down creating a balance pleasing to the spirit. This is grace then and how to view it.

Judgement
In stillness, as in contemplation, ones inner-light shines from within and what is real is clearly seen. The movements of the sun and stars inform us of the nature of time, while clear observance of the institutions formed within society provides the insight to improve ones community. For the superior man stillness has substance in clarity and clarity becomes functional through stillness.

Image
In contemplation we sense the world of ideals: the beauty of what could be in a perfect world. In this

state we transcend the conflict of the instincts but inevitably, we must return to the real world. When this happens we can use what we have learned from these archetypal ideas, but only in small matters.

The lines
First line

A beginner ought to learn to walk rather than be carried, otherwise many things will be missed. It is grace that makes this possible.

Second line

This line represents the quiet follower, whose only danger consists of a mild vanity. Acceptance of a lowly position, as for the first line, resolves this difficulty.

Third line

Here our first feeling of grace has left us overcome with drunkenness. Recognising that this is only an effect, and continuing to work toward the Good, resolves the difficulty that comes with the desire for more of the same feeling.

Fourth line

Doubt comes, concerning whether one should continue in contemplation as a lifestyle, or to return to the simple life the first line. While contemplation is a wonderful and undemanding experience, one remembers it is much more important to walk the walk like the first line.

Fifth line

The place of contemplation at the centre of ones being is unadorned and without complexity, therefore one can see clearly, without distraction. From here one recognises that one has only honest feeling to offer in any relationship.

Sixth line

The sincerity of ones nature and the sacrifice of all those below make it possible for one to achieve the grace of God. This means that one has accepted that, that which is real and simple, is the greatest form of progress.

23 Po – Splitting apart

Mountain over earth
Acceptance of fate.
The nature of acceptance is serenity
Ninth month October–November

Mountain over earth is the image of splitting apart.
The light line at the top is the ruler, but it is about to
be overthrown by the advancing darkness. This
hexagram symbolises autumn and the natural decline
of the life forces; also the attitude one should adopt as
the power of inferior people increases. A mountain is
formed as the earth splits and is driven upwards with
great energy, causing a rift. This energy, in the form of
fire, gradually cools and the top of the mountain is
left as a broken mass. In autumn fruit ripens and
splits, and the seeds fall to the ground in preparation
for Return. People, motivated by selfish objectives,
rise to power in darker times, and the only option for
the superior man is to accept the conditions gladly.

Judgement

The lower trigram and both nuclear trigrams are
K'un, the Devoted. Their energies, are submissive,
while the trigram of the ruling line, Chen means
Stillness. The overall inclination of the forces then, is
towards compliance with the situation. This implies
that though conditions appear unfavourable, due to
the exposed position, the safest place is amidst the
difficulties. In terms of character development, this is

a crucial phase, because one seems to be alone and without support. In such times, the threat seems so great, that fear can rise up from the depths of ones being and dominate the thoughts and reactions. The hexagram is a step by step procedure for dealing with these old responses, to life and death; decrease and increase.

Image

The mountain is pressed out of the earth and rests on a broad foundation. This is the outlook necessary for a superior character. The nature of the earth is to give everything, in order that the life cycle continues. The image of the mountain suggests contemplation of this. As a single image this implies the quality of view required at the time of greatest threat, and the willingness to give everything one has to those who have nothing. The top line is seen as the last piece of fruit on the tree. It cannot preserve itself, for this is not in the nature of things, but when it splits apart, the seed of new life falls to the ground. This image is analogous to the acceptance of ones destiny.

There is a further image not mentioned in other translations, which concerns the configuration of the lines. The shape of the lines might be viewed in many ways, but as regards the formation of character it depicts a state of serenity. The light line has risen to the top of the mountain where it can observe the approaching dark lines objectively. The five dark lines (broken lines) look like a channel, into which the light line can sink, and reappear at the foot of the hexagram, which then becomes 24 Return. The line makes the sacrifice, and sinks back into the crowd, because this conforms to its nature. The man of character withdraws from the masses at first, but only so that he can best see how to serve them.

The lines
First line

The first signs of splitting begin below the earth. The roots show signs of decay. In terms of society this suggests, that those people who have supported the ruler are in danger of being divided by negative forces.

Second line

Again, we have a situation where extreme forces are attempting to coerce the remaining supporters of the ruler. Here they have isolated them, in order to intimidate. Accept the isolation behaving as if one is in agreement. Wait quietly for support from friends, and then the threat can be avoided.

Third line

This line reacts instinctively to the evil that approaches it, and a conflict ensues. Because it has a direct correspondence, with the light line in the sixth place, it receives the strength it needs.

Fourth line

Because there is no light from the central line above it, the priest does not see the evil until it is upon him, and he is attacked directly. The only hope is that he can persevere until the light line returns.

Fifth line

The fifth line, the leader of dark lines, realises that the light power has not deserted them, and offers their support in his return. They will create a safe channel through which he can pass. This signifies that if one keeps a strong heart and open mind while under threat, the necessary spiritual strength can enter, and one will be able for the task.

Sixth line

Just as the last piece of fruit on a tree must eventually burst and release its seed, so the superior man exists, only so that he can pass on all that has been given to him. He accepts the offer of those below, as they create the path for his return. Because he is willing to return to the world of struggle, they welcome him with enthusiasm, and so paradoxically he is also a channel for their release from the evil which sought to isolate them.

24 Fu – Return

Earth over thunder
Thunder in the earth
December–January
The eleventh month, the month of the solstice
A turning point

Seven is the number of Return and occurs at the point of deepest darkness. Such a time is the Winter Solstice when the electrical power represented by thunder, resting within the earth, has begun to awaken. Awakening means, that the true returns as the false retreats.

Judgement

In this hexagram we can apprehend one of the primary ideas behind the I Ching; that all changes take place in their proper time. This occurs in six stages, the next stage, the seventh is called Return, and so solstices follow each other in the seventh month. All natural changes follow cyclic time and their results can be prophesied. Therefore, because the natural laws are reflected in man, his changes can also be predicted. This then is how the book of changes works, by following natural law. The sage-king finds that, in resting and allowing the life force to awaken quietly, he can observe its origin. Any act of self-will creates confusion, and the awareness and recognition of relationship with world and cosmos are lost. This hexagram therefore is of great importance regarding growth of character. In discerning the inner-light deep within, and its source, quieting the will becomes a profitable act. Knowing thyself means knowing the inner self.

Image
The light power that has withdrawn from the world in winter, returns at the darkest point though its effect is not yet apparent: the image of a snow-covered landscape, tranquil and unmoving; the world at rest while the spirit of life awakens invisibly below. The time of return is difficult to recognise, demands made by instinct and ego are strong, while the light of the spirit is only a potential. The smallest of mistakes can damage the life force, so it is wise to seek the aid of a genuine teacher.

The lines	*First line*

As the character strengthens itself in new ideas any thoughts of selfishly using this new energy must not be permitted to grow alongside. Like weeds these ideas are natural, but in the cultivation of character cannot be allowed to germinate.

Second line

At this level of understanding the sage-king observes the roots of old prejudices, again based upon selfish motives. These can be overcome only by a conscious decision to follow the principles of the group of like-minded individuals to whom one has been drawn. This opens the mind to the new possibilities within.

Third line

Where the instincts are powerful there is a tendency
to extreme behaviour patterns. These have control
because each extreme conveys the illusion that this is
the better way of life. When there is a threat to this
delusion, the movement is to the other extremity.
Nevertheless, because there is an honest desire to
change, it is likely that the defect will eventually be
overcome.

Fourth line

This is the line of the mediator or priest but as yet
there is no real inspiration, or fellowship in which to
fulfil one's role. The fourth line is directly connected
with the ruling line in the first place and so is able to
remain firm regarding its duty to spiritual principles.

Fifth line

This line represents the central place, the place of
greatest clarity. As it is a yin, or dark line, what is
imaged is the vision to see one's wrongs clearly and
without fear or favour. The necessary action is to
admit what one finds (as in confession), reducing the
dark or secret element, and in this way light returns to
the central core.

Sixth line

This place is one of great misfortune. Great because it
misses the time. Misfortune because it does so
arrogantly. Beset on all sides by wrong thoughts it
ignores the Way of the line below, to whom it feels
superior. Such an ego is driven to attain its will by
forceful and incomplete methods. Until it is humbled

in the manner of the first line it cannot become willing to turn about. The fact that this opportunity will come again in time is the only hope for such a personality.

25 Wu wang – Innocence
Heaven over thunder
The unexpected

Thunder, the voice of heaven, is about to make its first movement upward toward its proper place: a natural movement. Also, because it symbolises the first born returning to the father, we have the image of innocence. The lowest line is the son and the fifth line the father, therefore these lines rule the hexagram.

Judgement
This hexagram personifies the nature of man as essentially innocent, because he is a direct product of heaven. His deepest need is to be in harmony with, and to return to his primal nature. This is because at the centre of his being there resides the divine spirit, whose only desire is to follow will of God. The ego and the instincts tend to direct man away from the higher will and into a state of conflict and confusion. The only way back is to wait for the correct time i.e. when the dark forces are in retreat.

Image
Spring is the correct time for a return to innocence, because everything is renewed. The energies abroad are those of the life force seeking expression, and so are seen as sincere because there is nothing that is hidden or dark. The superior man in his speech is

simple and clear, in his actions he is natural and open so that those who follow his teachings will find their own simple natures.

The lines	*First line*

This line represents the power line of thunder, hidden beneath the earth. Its first movement is completely natural and intuitive and is to be trusted.

Second line

The work of the character of the second place is like that of the farmer as he directs the plow across the field. He simply follows the line of the last furrow, thinking neither of the work done, nor of the harvest to come. Because of this simple attitude fear and pride cannot obstruct him.

Third line

Unexpected difficulties can be costly if we react to them incorrectly. This line loses its placid demeanour and so misfortune is drawn to it. The solution is to seek out an attitude, consistent with acceptance of destiny, and return to the original innocence.

Fourth line

The honest nature of this line is not in jeopardy, but it has too much energy and others might try to lead it astray. An awareness of its simple duties is the only protection needed.

Fifth line

The central character channels the spiritual disease of others successfully, through himself, but sometimes these can manifest themselves as a physical malady.

These are best resolved through the medium of prayer, rather than resorting to medicines, which deal only with the symptoms.

Sixth line

Confusion and loss of balance are the result of consistently being in the wrong place at the wrong time. If we honestly wish to improve our characters it pays to sit quietly and review our position.

26 Ta ch'u – Taming power of the Great
Mountain over heaven

The fifth and sixth lines rule a powerful hexagram where the lower trigram heaven attempts to rise, but is blocked by the weight of the mountain. The energies of thunder and lake, the nuclear trigrams, are also held back by the stillness of the upper trigram, all of which connotes a build up of power in the hexagram as a whole. It is the yin lines, representing the ruler and mediator that press down upon the powerful forces of heaven. Their allegiance is to the ruler of the hexagram, at the top. Though the energies appear to be obstructed in their natural path, the hexagram is in truth exceptionally favourable, in that it depicts a storehouse of power.

Judgement
The storehouse symbolises the great man, who can replenish and strengthen his character on a daily basis via quiet meditation. During this time fresh energy flows into him, preparing him for the responsibilities of the day. This represents the sage figure at the top of the hexagram, whose obligations lead him to work directly with those in difficulty.

Image
The image of the mountain as a storehouse of hidden

wealth represents the manner in which all people might expand their spiritual lives. The practice of quietly contemplating the will of heaven at the beginning of each day, of asking for an understanding of this will, and finally acting upon it, are all suggested by this hexagram: speech and action by the nuclear trigrams of lake and thunder.

The lines
First line

The desire for immediate action must be controlled, as there is no clear path to ones goal. Quiet reflection, on all aspects of the situation, is likely to reveal a safe direction for the frustrated energies.

Second line

Movement for this line is also blocked, but because the character of this line is strong and aware, he recognises that it is his director in the fifth place who obstructs him. He waits with a calm spirit, and allows the energy to gather within him.

Third line

The obstacles to growth are removed for the third line, because it has direct contact with the sage at the top. The time for meditation is over and the duties of the day begin, but great care must be taken to avoid conflict with the yin lines. This loses nothing however, because it allows for practical use of the intuitions received during meditation.

Fourth line

The minister acts as the obstacle for undirected energies, in order that the sage can teach control and successful application.

Fifth line

This line also blocks the impatient force before its impetus can cause problems. If the energy of youth continues undisciplined, there must eventually be damage.

Sixth line

This line represents the great sage, whose energies are equal to the way of heaven. When a man has also a heavenly nature, he alters the way of man forever.

27 I – Corners of the mouth
Mountain over thunder
Nourishment

The lines of the hexagram provide the image of a mouth, with the first and sixth lines as lips, and those in between representing teeth. Nourishment passes through the mouth as food and words, both in and out. The mountain symbolises contemplation, stillness, while thunder stands for the voice of God and an upward movement. These together represent the motions of the mouth and at the same time, the act of speaking. This image depicts the idea of nourishment through the spoken word, nourishment for those seeking enlightenment.

Judgement
The judgement suggests that we analyse the nature of that which we nurture. If it is of the instincts or the ego then we feed our lower nature: if our efforts are for the nourishment of character and for others, then it is for our higher nature. The inference is of course, that the superior man nourishes his higher being by overcoming the desires of his lower nature.

Image
Thunder at the base of the mountain, moves slowly upward toward heaven. The superior man, in meditation, discerns that the presence of God in his

innermost being represents a spiritual hunger, and moderates his words and actions accordingly.

The lines   First line

This personality has the energy to improve itself, but chooses to depend on others to sustain him. This is an unnatural state, which arouses disgust in those around him, and eventually he finds himself without support or friendship.

Second line

A personality weakened by wrong living has to lean more and more upon others. This dependency creates a dis-ease of the soul, from which the only escape is a complete change of life-style.

Third line

When ones hunger is for spiritual satisfaction, and one seeks to satisfy it through other desires, there is a danger of creating a state of being, known in modern terms as addiction.

Fourth line

The true nature of the hunger is recognised by the minister. It is correct for him to seek guidance and strength from the top lines, because his need is to mediate for others.

Fifth line

Even though it is one of the ruling lines, this line lacks the power necessary for the work required of it. The line above has the essential attributes, as well as the will, and so the fifth line must reach out to it with humility for direction and support.

Sixth line

The character of this line is so advanced he is described as a sage-king. There are great dangers for a man of such strength, especially in an exposed position, but self-awareness and willingness for the work protect him.

28 Ta kuo – Preponderance of the Great
Mountain over heaven

This hexagram is dominated from the inside by yang lines, which is not their proper place. When light lines are on the outside, they have freedom of movement, and are also in a position to protect the weaker yin lines. When there is a build up of energy at the centre, the extremes will suffer from an overload and burn out. This extraordinary situation comes about because of the complacency that comes with a fine life. Above is the trigram which denotes joy, and below the gentle energy of wind. This happy attitude creates an illusory state, trapping the creative energy inside, which eventually reaches overload.

Judgement
The active power of the creative is expressed in the world of men as spiritual energy, and through the superior man as duty, but an excess occurs when there is a lack of activity. The individual lines of the hexagram suggest the various ways of expending this energy to avoid a collapse. Despite the suggestion of complacency, the situation is viewed as a natural eventuality in the life of the sage, which occurs at a time of greater expansion: new avenues need to be found for the excess of power one is about to receive.

Image

The image describes the attitude necessary to avoid collapse, and prepare for the distinctive changes about to be experienced. Spiritual sustenance, symbolised by the lake water, has risen over the tree because it has had no outlet, but the tree stands strong and awaits its destiny. This describes how the spiritual man accepts the changes in his life controlled by fate: he is willing to give up the world in favour of doing what is correct.

The lines   *First line*

At times of extraordinary change it is vital that we behave with care at the beginning, so that when the alterations have come about there need be no remorse.

Second line

The image for the second line is that of a man with a young wife. This represents the new viewpoint that comes when ones energies are revitalised. For the man of character, this suggests that he should begin working with those people who have waiting for his assistance, and in this way his essential energies are renewed.

Third line

The personality of this line suffers from blind obstinacy. He insists on dealing with the obvious difficulties aggressively, and so the beneficial changes do not come to him. Because he must continuously fail his world collapses, and he is left alone and afraid.

There is a possibility that this humiliation might alter his point of view and enable him to make a beginning.

Fourth line

Because what we are looking for is a new attitude, we must let go of the old one, but if we attempt to use those gifts we receive as mediators for ourselves, then we lose them. This is the ruling line and is aware of the dangers, but it is suggested that he discuss the situation with the first line, which is also the ruler.

Fifth line

This line has for its image a young husband and an older wife. Though the marriage will have no progeny there is no judgement on the situation, but in terms of character development it translates into a refusal to let go of our old ideas.

Sixth line

This line represents the idea behind the hexagram as a whole. Once the water has risen over the trees there is no more to be done. We have tried to make all of the changes necessary in the correct manner, but even these are not sufficient and we are overwhelmed. This represents the courage of the man who is willing to go all the way in favour of doing what is right, even at the cost of his life.

29 K'an – The Abysmal
Water over water
Doubled trigram
The middle son

The central yang lines rule the hexagram. The symbolism of water above and below is that of the cycle of rain in the heavens and in the oceans, forever changing place. It also represents the cycle of spirit. Beginning in heaven it is dispensed below returning to source and then back again into the world. Regarding the lines, a yang line flows between yin lines, like a river of energy at the centre of being. Also the symbol of a river flowing through the deep abyss, from which comes the attribute of danger. To free oneself from the danger, we need to move as independently and smoothly as the river.

Judgement
The hexagram really represents the actions we should take to avoid the consequences of danger. What is suggested is that if we behave in the manner of water, which is that it follows its nature; it flows freely over and under all obstacles; and wears down the greatest of obstructions. The parallel for the spiritual man is that, once he has attained his true nature, he can move freely through the world, as long as he remains sincere to his greater self. These dangers come mostly from within, from the enticements of the lower self.

Image

The greatest quality of water is that it is eternally changing, without ever losing its true nature. It brings life to the world by entering all things, then returns to source to begin the cycle again. In this way it symbolises the life force, which follows the same cycle, never losing its character. The sage follows the example of water by remaining sincere to his nature, under all conditions, and persevering toward the good. He applies the example with the use of repetition in his teaching.

The lines	*First line*

Water flows over and through and never lingers, in this way it avoids being trapped. If we hesitate in our forward movement and become fascinated by the feel of danger, we become addicted to excitement, an addiction that cannot be satisfied. It is only when evil is so close we can smell it that we recognise the true danger, but by then we are trapped like water in a pit.

Second line

This line is enthusiastic to do great things, but danger is all around and so a complete analysis of the situation is required. When an intelligent strategy has been formed, and if the time is correct, an escape will be formulated.

Third line

The desire to escape is strong for this line, but quicksand is all around. As with the second line, patience is required until a safe path can be found. It is essential to ignore the voice of the instincts at this time.

Fourth line

The minister reaches out to the ruler of the hexagram, the strong character in the line above. Because of the dangerous situation he does this directly, and without the usual social graces, and his help is accepted. In times of common threat it pays to concentrate on a way out, rather than the superficial rules of society.

Fifth line

Like attracts like, and if we live a self-serving existence, evil seeks us out. The central character avoids making his presence known when evil is close, and seeks only to extricate himself and those in his charge from the threat at hand.

Sixth line

The extreme personality is encircled by the cruelty of his past actions, from which there is no escape for at least three years. The term of three years was for a grave offence and suggests an inability to repent or reform.

30 Li – The Clinging Tree

Fire over fire
Fire doubled – the image of time

In this doubled hexagram, the trigrams of fire represent the continuous movement of the sun and the concept of time. Fire depicts the dependency between the light and dark principles, through which the nature of both becomes manifest. Flame, being formless, perseveres only if there is substance at its centre, just as the light of life when manifest through growing things, is dependent on the world. The second and fifth lines, both yin, are the rulers because they hold the central places.

Judgement
The dependent aspect of fire demonstrates how man's nature is conditioned by the physical limitations of his world. From this understanding comes a recognition, that there is also a dependency on cosmic and spiritual forces, and that dependencies of this kind are both natural and beneficent. Knowing this creates the inner clarity for spiritual development, and therefore for an ever-expanding influence.

Image
Flame presses upward and is seen from a great distance. The character of the superior man, when attuned to its nature is bright and enduring. His

teaching is equal to his practice: illuminate the inner being and the outer world becomes clear.

The lines
First line

This line exemplifies the first awakening of the spirit, when demands from the outside world overshadow the inner clarity. The suggestion for this line is to begin each morning with a quiet time, in order to prepare for many confusions of the day.

Second line

This line shows the benefits of the middle way. Rejecting all extremes this line is in harmony with its nature. As with the light of the sun at noon, everything is clear.

Third line

Twilight has an illusory quality, which awakens extreme reactions in some people. Reminded that life also comes to an end, they can get drunk or sink into depression. The solution is to reject the emotional response, and accept the reality of the transitoriness of life.

Fourth line

This line behaves like a brush fire or shooting star, in that it burns but with short duration. The character depicted here ought not to burn in all directions at once, rather it should follow a single purpose.

Fifth line

This is the high point of a career, where successes have brought great acclaim. It would be easy to bask in the glow of such approval, but the character of this line has enough clarity to recognise the vanity of such an illusion.

Sixth line

This line represents the warlord of the prince below. It falls to him to produce a strategy, whose aims are to remove those forces, which stand in the way of positive growth.

31 Hsien – Influence

Lake over mountain
Lake is the youngest daughter – mountain the youngest son

The fourth and fifth lines rule the hexagram through their influence on others, the former through the heart and the latter via the unconscious mind. The trigrams are the youngest son and the youngest daughter, whose influence on each other represents the affinity between the sexes, in a non-specific manner. The male courts the female by standing below her with courtesy and respect, and she in turn courts him by joyously accepting his advances.

Judgement

Lake and mountain stimulate each other, in the same way that the complimentary energies of male and female are drawn together. The steady influence of the male attracts the female, and she favours him with her joyous response. The sage influences others into happily following his example, a happiness that stimulates him to continue his work.

Image

The mountain attracts clouds to its summit and rain fills the hollow, and a lake is formed. Through mutual attraction, life on the mountain is nourished and the lake is regularly replenished. In the same way the sage appeals to people who perceive humility as a virtue:

they approach him because he nourishes their
spiritual needs without ego.

The lines   *First line*

Movement begins in the toes but the world is not
affected, and so there is no judgement regarding this.
Only when there is an influence can we judge our
actions to be real.

Second line

This yin line ought to wait to be called by the central
character in the fifth place, with whom it has a
connection. If it is impatient and chooses to take
action with the lower line it will come to grief.

Third line

The instinctive behaviour of this personality is his
downfall, because he feels that he must be stimulated
at all times. The lower lines tempt him from his goal
by appealing to its vanity. If he can rise above this
dangerous conduct he will have achieved something
in his character.

Fourth line

Worry and inner torment come from consciously
controlling people and situations. The nature of the
superior man is to follow his duty without concern for
the outcome, or for the illusion of praise. Vanity
cannot be satisfied but humility is its own reward.

Fifth line

The unconscious mind controls much of our being
without our knowledge of it, but the sage enters the
secret depths of his mind and allows himself to be

influenced. He does this by stilling the rational thoughts through meditation, then shares the intuitions with his fellows.

Sixth line

Gossip has an appeal for a while and only for a superficial type of person, but even they depart after a while, and seek some other stimulation.

32 Heng – Duration

Thunder over Wind
Endurance

The flexible nature of wind inside, and the vitality of thunder outside, defines the way of endurance. A strong forward movement balanced by a gentle, yet penetrating attitude, suggests an influence that endures through time. That which gives duration to one thing also provides the potential for this quality in all things. If we can recognise, through contemplation, the essential laws within the former then it becomes possible to endure in all situations by adjusting to their formula.

Yin and yang refer to the light and dark, the two primal powers of Nature. This means that the lines and hexagrams are symbols for these powers, and so the I Ching is a demonstration that the nature of the universe is eternity, and that the universe is in a constant state of flux. This principle, of constant change, applies also to man and the world.

Judgements

The movements of stars and galaxies are constant, just as the actions of the solar system follow a continuous regularity. It is the laws behind their regulation, which provide endurance. These laws apply to the seasons so that life too endures. To reproduce these laws within oneself it is necessary to follow the path of constant change inherent in ones nature. This primary directive is called the Tao or the Way.

Image
The image of unity in constant movement and change provides the image of the qualities required for strength of character. A mind, open to the needs of the time, and a willingness to submit to the influences of change, are the prerequisites for this firmness to come about.

The lines   *First line*

When we first seek to possess endurance we do so in a reckless manner, in an attempt to forego those changes that we would rather not face. This can only bring remorse and frustration, which in the long run are equally as painful as the difficulties we are trying to avoid.

Second line

This is the controlling line because it is in a central place and in correspondence with the six in the fifth place. Despite having strength of character, the physical resources are insufficient for the task. The character will be strengthened by an act of self-control in this situation.

Third line

Here we have a character lacking in stamina and therefore powerless against the instinctive drives. Repeated humiliations divert from the primary direction, resulting in a cycle of discontent. This creates a desire for a satisfactory outcome and more remorse. (Continuous attempts by the instincts to overpower the will are one way that character defects are formed.) The cycle can only be broken by an appeal to the Good within, in the hope that a better purpose will lead to endurance. This line is in correspondence with the six at the top, which is also weak and therefore unable to offer strength.

Fourth line

There is an ignorance about the source of inner strength predominant in those of a strong will. This arrogance tempts them into a downward spiral of defeats and humiliations. It is only at the point of deepest despair that such a will might find redemption, and the beginnings of a character possessing true endurance.

Fifth line

From this line we can learn about the nature of the energies within. The yin or female power is gentle and supportive, while the yang energy is expressive and directive. This is imaged in the uniting of wind with thunder and expressed in the correspondence of the second and fifth lines. When the central line has a yin nature it suggests a flexible attitude toward situations, which can change at any moment.

Sixth line

This place has no strength of character whatsoever. It represents a mind that is never still, and so is unable to find satisfaction. Because of this state of restlessness it is incapable of focus, and is tempted

further and further from the centre. As with line three
the only solution lies in a movement toward the
Good.

33 Tun – Retreat

Heaven over mountain
Sixth month July–August

This hexagram represents a time when the practice of self-restraint becomes necessary in order to preserve the vital energies accumulated. Mountain represents quietness within, while heaven represents the place and principles of the spirit. This symbolises the withdrawal of the attributes of the higher self from the forces of the lower self, which seek to overpower them. This parallels the beginning of winter when the light withdraws as darkness moves closer. The fifth line rules the hexagram.

Judgement

The importance of this hexagram lies in good timing. The encroachment of darkness as winter approaches is a natural event. There is no conflict between light and dark, only an acceptance of the time by the forces of light. Therefore the retreat is be orderly and controlled in which neither force is damaged. The sage uses this image to improve his strategy, while gaining a deeper understanding of character. He does not engage in conflict, neither does he take flight. He withdraws to a safe distance in order to observe the situation, and plan his movements.

Image

The mountain personifies a lower point of view, while heaven is expansive. The image of retreat, the one from the other, symbolises the withdrawal of the higher faculties from those of the lower i.e. the character from the personality.

The lines
First line

This line is the closest to the enemy's front line and so its strategy is to be invisible. When one is pursued it pays to detach and observe the situation.

Second line

The second line is central but weak and seeks to join with a strong line, but the fifth line is also weak, and the third line, which is strong, is impulsive.

Therefore the only recourse is to continue in what is right, even though this means suffering loneliness for a while.

Third line

This instinctive personality is always impatient. Weak when strength is needed and inflexible when the time calls for sensitivity. Only when exhausted is he able to stop, but if he evaluates his condition honestly at these times, there is the possibility of change.

Fourth line

The minister is able to accept retreat happily, for he knows nothing is lost. Only the inferior personality suffers from bruised pride when he must withdraw.

Fifth line

The central character knows the true from the false.

He also knows when it is time to withdraw and does so without any qualms.

Sixth line

The line at the top receives the benefits of total withdrawal from the negative elements. This richness is the result of careful detachment from the temptations of ego and desire, and is the beginning of a new freedom and a new happiness.

34 Ta chuang – Power of the Great
Thunder in heaven

The fourth strong line is the ruler in a powerful hexagram. The energy of heaven in the lower trigram drives upwards, and Thunder the voice of God, above it moves in like manner. The four yang lines together are the ridgepoles of God's house, holding back the storm of chaos, represented by the yin lines.

Judgement
With such an abundance of energy it would be easy to be overwhelmed by the belief that we can accomplish anything. Such an attitude leads only to errors and waste of spiritual force, which is given to achieve something of greatness. It is necessary to hesitate before taking any reckless action, listening for the inner voice symbolised by the upper trigram, in order to conform to what is right. The fourth line is the ruler, which suggests that we seek counsel from a mediator concerning intuitions we might receive.

Image
In spring thunder rises from the ground in the form of electrical energy, exploding to create shock waves, which can be heard and felt at great distances. Such an influence, delivered in a way in complete accord with nature and heaven, personifies something great, such

as the voice of God.

The lines *First line*

This line represents the first movement, which is in the toes. Because of the energy involved, there is likely to be wilful action and so we are told to be on guard for mistakes, and to practise self-restraint.

Second line

The strong line depicted here has much inner resolve and so is unlikely to act excessively, yet there is a warning not to be fooled by the ease with which obstacles are overcome, for this would lead to dangerous complacency.

Third line

Despite the strength of the instincts usually found in the third place, this line is easily able to control the desire to abuse the power given to it.

Fourth line

All obstacles to character growth and spiritual harmony have disintegrated, as a result of persistent work towards their removal. This is the secret of true success- to be persevering in working on ones own character.

Fifth line

The only real block to personal improvement is a prejudicial attitude based on contempt, but because of the support of the lower lines, this line is able to let go of this serious defect and move forward.

Sixth line

This line represents a situation where one has become

trapped by stubbornness, and unlike the line below, can find no way out. The solution is simple, it is only a case of surrendering completely, and reaching out for help to the strong lines beneath.

35 Chin – Progress
Fire over Earth

In the hexagram of fire rising above the world, progress is imaged as the sun, climbing swiftly to its zenith. This represents a point of view expanding continuously, in the manner of light covering more and more of the earth.

Judgement
Progress within the social order transpires when a leader appears, who is both willing to follow his superior without question, and also lead his fellows in the service of this ruler. This results in favour for all, in that gifts are bestowed downwards upon those willing to unite in such a way. In terms of character, this implies a stage where one has become wise enough to recognise that, to lead, one must first learn to serve. This means the honesty and open-mindedness of the sage with regard to his dealings with others.

Image
The nature of light is clarity, just as the nature of man is innately good. The dawn light is red as the rays of sun encounter toxic materials in the atmosphere. This is unavoidable, in the same way that the nature of man becomes shadowed by his interaction with

mundane things. This is the way of existence, but in this hexagram we are shown how to make progress toward the Good by removing the negative effects, which are a block to refining the character. Cultivating character requires the clearing away of useless materials, in order to allow the light at the centre to shine through.

The lines   *First line*

Here the suggestion is to hesitate in ones efforts for progress. This might be due to the possibility of rejection from those we would wish to help, or simply because the time is not yet right. Still, nothing is lost for we can continue with other work until a more propitious time.

Second line

We need help from the central character in the fifth place, but as with the line below, we are blocked. We should neither panic nor force the issue. Progress here comes from persevering alone until the way is clear.

Third line

At the head of the lower trigram, this line makes progress because it has the willing support of those below. Their example outlines the true nature of progress, which is that of great sacrifice in favour of the good of all.

Fourth line

This line is a warning against behaving in a manner in opposition to those in a lowly position. Work for ones own advantage, at a cost to those in ones community, is always done in the shadows, but the light falls on good and evil without favour. Eventually they must observe one another. Such actions, by their nature, always result in isolation.

Fifth line

This line, the primary, describes how a gentle personality behaves as the leader of a fellowship having connections with the sovereign. Such a character is able to view success and failure as one thing, and not be hindered by the confusion that results from these dilemmas. Other people feel able to approach with their difficulties, because they feel they will be heard without prejudice.

Sixth line

This line suggests aggressive progress. While it may be necessary to discipline those in ones immediate fellowship, to do so with those who are not would lead to no advancement whatsoever. Due to the isolation of this position, it is safer to work vigorously on ones own defects and progress in this way.

36 Ming i – Darkening
Earth over fire

It is night and the world is perceived as rising above the sun. This provides an image of a dark personality, in a position to control the movements of the sage-king. The central lines in the second and fifth places, both yin are the rulers of the hexagram, and it is they who are oppressed by the shadowy personality.

Judgement
The trigrams also represent the fire hidden within the earth, which represents the will of the sage-king at times of oppression. He hides his true power until the moment his enemy is at his weakest, when he can act with the strength of fire bursting from the ground. The lines depict the action to be taken in order to protect the Inner Light from serious damage.

Image
The image of light within the earth is used to portray a natural situation, (natural because both good and evil are perceived as behaving according to their nature), where the forces of darkness are ascendant. During these times it is necessary that we behave in a prudent manner, avoiding any direct conflict, which might draw the destructive forces in our direction. This is not to suggest that our conduct should be

anything but exemplary, only that a wise strategy does not include throwing oneself away needlessly.

The lines   First line

At the first sign of conflict the superior man attempts to rise above it, but darkness is all around and so he seeks to withdraw, but again is set on from all sides. The pressure is on to make a compromise, to meet the opposing forces halfway, but to do so would just be the first of many concessions, which would eventually result in total capitulation. There is no recourse but to become a wanderer, working anonymously toward the good. In this way his principles are safeguarded, though he forfeits support and comfort to do so.

Second line

The shadowy personality causes direct injury to the character of the sage-king, but the wound has no effect. Instead it spurs him on to protect others who might be affected. Paradoxically, it is this selfless act which neutralises the damage.

Third line

This line usually creates its own problems because of its extreme reactions, but the character has become so strong that it has the troublesome instincts under control. As much work has already been done in this area, it seems like coincidence that the tyrant of self-will reappears, but the superior character knows that there are always hidden avenues within the self. Because of his constant awareness, he is able to apprehend the shadowy personality before any damage is caused.

Fourth line

The dark presence is so close that we can perceive his intent, and recognising that there is no capacity for the light of truth, we withdraw.

Fifth line

This is the central character, the sage-king, mentioned in the judgement who hides his strength until the dark enemy has exhausted himself, and then returns like the sun at dawn, to take his rightful place and lead the world out of darkness.

Sixth line

The top line depicts the manner in which darkness is always defeated: having overcome the light forces completely there is nothing on which it might feed and is defeated by its own appetite. In terms of character development, this describes the unique strategy of the superior man, who withdraws all support from those destructive traits that appear unexpectedly, and attempt to usurp control.

37 Chia jen – The Family

Wind over Fire
The nature of yin is seen through traditions

The hexagram as a whole outlines the respective
duties of the family, each line representing a different
family member. The trigrams symbolise the influence
of the family on the world at large. Fire, meaning
clarity, spreads its influence through wind, which it
creates by its energy. In the same way the family, when
harmonious and productive, spreads these same
qualities to the rest of society.

In the individual lines we perceive the patriarchal
society, based on the qualities of yin and yang,
prevalent in Chinese society. The energies of the
trigrams are female, therefore we see that the
controlling power of the family as traditional.

Judgement

The second and fifth lines, that is the wife and
husband, are the rulers of the hexagram, and of
themselves represent the correct places assigned for
their respective powers. Yin represents the power of
tradition and is within, whereas yang represents duty
and is outside. What is made clear in this hexagram is
that the responsibility for the success of social order
falls on the family not on those who rule. The family
of the body, which means its vital energies, is
controlled by the human mind. Because this is

conditioned it is always discontented, wasting the vital energies. Refining the self means removing the conditioned mind.

Image
Just as the influence of the family unit projects outwards into society, so should its example of balance and correct behaviour, be practised by each individual member. If others observe that what we say is not what we do, then what we say will fall on deaf ears.

The lines   *First line*
Here is the place of the youngest son, whose duty is to emulate the code of proper behaviour, practised by the family as a whole. His example comes from the older brother, who he imitates through affection, and from the father, who he imitates through love. The mother provides the content and the father provides the firmness. In terms of personal growth, it is easier for the will to be altered before it has become stubborn.

Second line
This line represents the mother image, the central force within the family. She provides the content, which is tradition. From this position she also provides social and religious substance for the community as a whole. The implication is to observe the nature of ones abilities and adhere to these. Fulfil those duties, which are immediate.

Third line

Here difficulties arise between the mother and son.
Because their natures are different, the mother is
unsure about discipline. The suggestion is that it is
better to give too much than too little. In personal
terms the indication is that one can always apologise
for ones over-reactions and be forgiven, but it is
impractical to attempt to bring discipline up to the
mark when we have been too lenient.

Fourth line

Again we have image of the female member of the
house, the older sister, who carries the treasures, or
the traditions, of the family. The nature of the family
endures, through the perpetuation of the traditional
element of family life. The essence of this line is
devotion to the well being of others.

Fifth line

This is the ruling line and the place of the husband.
His duty is to improve his character, for if his
influence is incorrect, how can the rest of the family
behave with love and trust? This applies to all who
draw this line.

Sixth line

This is the line of the father also, but pertains to the
man able to make the sacrifices necessary to achieve a
character, which honours others.

38 K'uei – Opposition
Fire over lake
Opposition means there are differences

The rulers are in the second and fifth places and it is their duty to work toward reconciliation. Fire and water conflict in their natures: flame reaches upward toward heaven and the lake fills the lowly spaces. Further to this idea of going separate ways, the trigrams represent the second and third daughters, who leave the family home when they marry, so that their interests diverge. It is the qualities of their personalities that can save the relationship: the lake symbolises union, and fire has clarity able to see beyond differences of opinion.

Judgement
The meaning of the hexagram is outlined through the difficulties experienced by people of opposing natures. Fire and water are symbolic of these, but we might also observe the differences between the sun and the earth, and the world of the spirit in opposition to the world of nature. These are complementary opposites, representing the extremes of yin and yang, and so opposition is really only the tension through which all life is created. The superior man has balance in his life, because he accepts the extremes within his nature without conflict.

Image

Opposition is removed because the qualities within the trigrams are compatible, but despite the reunion both elements always preserve their original natures. The work of the sage man brings him into contact with people of all types, but his behaviour always reflects his nature not theirs.

The lines	*First line*

Everything belonging to man's nature returns to him eventually, of its own accord, just as all that is not of his nature, must leave. Because of this law we need not waste energy clinging to things or driving them away.

Second line

The strength of character of this line shows through great patience. Rather than hurry into a premature reconciliation it waits, until the friend in the fifth place approaches or until there is a chance meeting.

Third line

The man of instincts has a different outlook to the egoist, and so the personality of this line reacts with self-pity when his friend, represented by the top line, rejects him. If he sacrifices his own viewpoint, the conflict can be resolved.

Fourth line

The situation surrounding this personality is one of conflict, due to pressure from people of different extremes, but if he can remove the difficulties between himself and his friend in the first line, all other blockages are eliminated.

Fifth line

It is the duty of this line to approach the yang line in the second place from which it has been parted. When this is done the problems between them are healed almost of themselves.

Sixth line

The egoist tends toward a superior manner, and in this case harm has been caused to the companion in the third place. A different perspective is required because the hurt party is approaching, with a helpful and forgiving attitude.

39 Chien – Obstruction
Water over mountain

The barrier to forward movement is a crevasse full of water, while behind us is a wall of solid rock. The only alternative is to seek refuge at the foot of the mountain, and when there to be still, contemplating the nature of the problem.

Judgement
It is this act of quietly reviewing the situation that leads to the removal of the blockage. When faced with a dangerous and apparently unalterable situation, we need to construct a strategy equal to the condition. We should know our own strengths and weaknesses, as well as those pertaining to the obstruction. Having made our calculations, we should then humbly ask for as much help as is required to overcome the problem. The sage observes the difficulty and looks for its reflection within himself, and so all adversities lead to character development.

Image
Danger and frustration result from extreme difficulties, so we must first quieten these reactions or we are blinded to their true nature. The solution to an unalterable situation is to alter our perspective toward it, to marshal all of our forces, and surmount the

problem. The lines represent the various factors of the obstruction, which personal energies are involved, and the new attitude required to alter the situation.

The lines	*First line*

The first line represents the lower limbs and so depicts action, but in this case we must walk backwards to a place of safety. From our vantagepoint we can review the situation clearly and see where the fault is within us.

Second line

Despite careful consideration the character of this line enters the area of danger. This appears to be a mistake, but there is a direct connection with the sage in the fifth place who is surrounded by dangerous pits. This totally unselfish attitude is all that protects him from falling into the traps himself.

Third line

The character of the man of instincts is stronger than his wilder impulses in this case, and he is able yield to the new impressions that come to him. Instead of rushing blindly ahead he retreats to the mutual protection of his family and group.

Fourth line

It falls to this line to make the analysis of the situation: to calculate assets and defects, to evaluate honestly the chances of success and failure, and to accept completely the information discovered. Having done this it is necessary to share the findings with those above and below, and to wait for the proper time to act.

Fifth line

The character of the fifth line represents the higher self at the centre of being to which everything of our true nature flows. This is the central character, or the image of God, who gathers and deploys the energies so that all difficulties can be overcome. In the same way the leader of a fellowship or group can rest in the middle of danger, and quietly organise an intelligent strategy. In this way everyone benefits as they emulate his courage and quietness, and all are able to observe and remove the obstacles to clarity and insight.

Sixth line

The top line is beyond the difficulties: the obstacles no longer apply and so he need not return to them. His duty, however, demands that he go back through the dangerous country and offer his allegiance to the central character. The experience of a man who has transcended ego is essential in a situation where clear vision is required.

40 Hsieh – Deliverance
Thunder over water
After the storm the channels are full

When blockages are removed, the channel is clear and the river flows freely. This does not mean that the danger is eliminated, however, in fact a further hazard, a fast moving flood, has been added. The warning, that one should not allow energy released to carry one away carelessly, is difficult to be mindful of in the first moments of freedom, but must be obeyed as soon as possible. This is not all of the danger, for though the barriers have been broken up there will still be fragments of the original problem, caught up in a variety of ways. These too must be sought out and removed.

Judgement
The ruling lines are the second and fifth. The second line is yang, and therefore active. Once its work has been done, it returns to the centre to rest. The fifth line is yin and liberates itself, and in doing so proves its worth to all. (A parallel idea might be, 'Physician heal thyself!') These two represent the work that must be done, in order to accomplish a complete release from the initial difficulties. Where this applies to social problems, it demonstrates the way in which a community works as a team to remove the last vestiges of old problems. Those who do not help, tend

to be washed away in the flood.

Image

Thunder comes and the storm removes tension, rain falls and blockages are forcibly removed from the river channel. This is the image of deliverance. The ruler resolves social tensions by forgiving the intended wrongs and forgetting those that grow from personal weakness. When this concerns his own character, he strengthens his resolve in working toward the good, knowing that his own defects will be washed away in the flood of energy so released.

The lines	*First line*

In the first moments of deliverance, those who have worked hard toward this moment should rest. There is more work ahead, and it will be better faced with a renewed energy and a happy heart.

Second line

In the final removal of the obstacles to growth and forward movement, one is faced with entities hiding behind the obstruction. These are simple vanities, whether they appear in ones community, or defects of character. Working toward their removal is the only way to remove their seductiveness.

Third line

Here, the vanity mentioned below has taken root. Being freed from the poverty of his past, this man is instinctively driven to seek the comfort he feels is due to him. This is a mistake, because he has only succeeded in breaking up the manifestation of his problem. The true nature of his blocks now ought to be dealt with, in order that they are not reconstructed.

Fourth line

It is the job of this line to provide directions for those who desire to work toward the good, or to reinforce their position. There are those who, for selfish reasons, helped in the removal of the initial problem and now expect a free ride. Their pleas must be ignored, for they are in reality, a manifestation of the very difficulties one is now attempting to overcome.

Fifth line

The ruling line shows an attitude of gentleness, which the strong lines are attracted to, recognising its humility. But weaker individuals see this quality as feebleness and are persistent in their demands. This is the line, which liberates itself, and does so by withdrawing from the dependency of those around him. To do this, he must withdraw from his own dependencies and forgive his own defects.

Sixth line

The last remnant of the blockage has come to rest in the highest position. Strengthened by the forces of habit, this entity has the power to cling to every thought, to prey upon every positive motivation. Like a hawk, hidden in the shadows of the castle battlements, it cannot be seen, but watches everything. Locked into the ego, vanity waits to swoop on the unwary. One must prepare oneself well before attempting to shoot this predator.

41 Sun – Decrease
Mountain over lake
Decrease represents cultivating character

The fifth line rules in a hexagram that, at first sight, might appear detrimental. But decrease is viewed as a natural condition, without which, things would become too full. The lake loses some of its water as mist rises, nourishing life on the mountain. The lake symbolises the passion, and the mountain is the symbol of explosive rage: we discipline desires by limiting their control over our lives, while rage is diminished by the practice of quiet contemplation. In this way we decrease the powers of the lower self to benefit the higher. Also imaged is the decrease in wealth of the lower classes to profit the government, for instance in the form of taxes, in order that the society and its structure can be improved.

Judgement
When the members of a community have a good standard of living but the communal coffers are empty, it is time to increase taxes. If the people judge their wealth selfishly, there is likely to be a backlash, but the governing party cannot ignore the situation to increase favour with the people. There are times also when individuals must sacrifice personal gratification, to increase the spiritual comfort of the community as a whole.

Image

As the mist rises to the top of the mountain, all of life is enriched, but the change in the lake is hardly discernible. At the time of decrease, it is the willingness to change that is significant, because there is no real loss. When small sacrifices are made in the worldly sense, the increase is felt in the world of the spirit. This is how to cultivate character development.

The lines   *First line*

Giving unselfishly requires great insight. For instance we should not give so much that those who depend on us suffer deprivation, nor should we give so much that we suffer resentment or hatred. In other words we should give enough to improve our characters, not strengthen our negative drives. A hint is given also concerning the art of unselfish taking, which also requires sacrifice and insight. If we consciously take more than the other can afford, then we decrease ourselves in terms of character.

Second line

The strength of character of this line demands that the giving be dignified, for if we give only to improve our social standing, then, as with the first line, we only increase the lower self.

Third line

When three people spend time together, one must eventually leave or difficult situations arise and negative emotions ensue. The yang line has journeyed to the top of the mountain, and the yin line has taken its place, causing fresh difficulties, and so this line looks to the line at the top for friendship. This means that the sacrifice has been made and inner harmony is achieved.

Fourth line

The defects of character blocking this personality from the company of others are those pertaining to social differences, and so those of lower rank who would aid in his improvement cannot approach him. His only hope is a willingness to change, that comes from an honest analysis of his problems.

Fifth line

The central character is the representative of heaven, or the image of God, and needs only to fulfil his destiny to achieve harmony and balance for himself and those he serves.

Sixth line

This line represents the sage who is no longer a part of the community, meaning he has no property and nowhere to lay his head. The third line, whose character is strengthened by unselfish sacrifice, aids him as a friend and follower. This describes how the superior character increases others, through the increase that comes to him from heaven.

42 I – Increase
Wind over thunder
Increase represents the time when character is full.

The fifth and second lines rule because their
characters are central and appropriate, in every sense.
Whereas, in the preceding hexagram, the upper
trigram increased because of a sacrifice of the lower,
in the hexagram of increase the sacrifice is on the part
of the upper trigram. Heaven has sent its
representative to sink into the earth and its breath to
fill the skies. Thunder the eldest son, and wind
representing the eldest daughter, are formed and
brought together by an act of self-sacrifice on the part
of heaven. The world of the spirit enters the world of
the senses and both are improved.

Judgement
When the communal coffers are overflowing, the
government releases wealth into the community and a
time of social expansion occurs. In terms of spiritual
development, society increases because of the wealth
of good feeling and fellowship that comes when the
time of poverty is ended. The superior man works
toward the good with the power of thunder, removing
his defects becoming flexible as wind, and so finds his
original nature. This is his example to those who
follow him.

Image

Thunder and wind work together to remove the
tension of chaotic energies: the wind symbolically
carries thunder, the message of God, to great
distances. The meaning of the time of increase and
decrease is reflected in the waxing and waning of the
sun and moon: all things reach fullness and then
change to their complementary opposites. Goodness
increases because we reduce defects. To increase
goodness further requires a further decrease of
defects.

The lines   *First line*

The minister in the fourth place strengthens the first
line, and so his motivations to act are correct.
Increase for this line comes from an honest
connection with a spiritual guide.

Second line

A yin line in a yin place means that it is receptive to
the power of good and cognisant of its natural
qualities, and because of this it knows what can be
decreased and increased. Harmony of energies comes
from knowing the demands of the time, and how they
hold the seeds of the future.

Third line

At the time of increase even those with extreme
personalities can prosper, but only if they are willing
to alter and grow through an honest confession of
their defects, and to help others to cultivate character
growth in the same way.

Fourth line

A minister ought to be objective in the work of
mediating between God and man, ruler and
community, but this attitude leads to claims of
disinterest and lack of compassion. If we are to teach
anything of character improvement, we need to
harden ourselves against slander, and engage the
support of those who have gone before us. Engaged in
a fellowship where all are connected by honesty,
means that all are increased though the power of
truth.

Fifth line

The central character follows the path of duty, and has
a compassionate heart. Through compassion and
honesty he attracts those who are unfortunate, and
teaches them the art of expansion, in order that they
in their turn become teachers.

Sixth line

The personality, who attempts to teach expansion
before he has worked on his own defects, is an affront
to everyone. Whatever his motivation, it will be
defective and therefore dishonest and self-serving.
How can he bring anything but more chaos? The rule
of heaven and man is that we cannot confess the
defects of others, only our own.

43 Kuai – Breakthrough

Lake over Heaven
April–May
Third month
A clear channel

This hexagram depicts the end of a time of great difficulty, when the pressure that built up as a result, is about to be released. Because of sustained action, negative forces have been pushed out, leaving the channel almost completely clear. The sky is heavy with clouds, and the water lifted from the lake is about to fall as rain. Another image is that of the constant pressure placed upon negative character traits by creative energies. One final movement is required, but this must be taken in a legitimate manner or all past efforts will have been in vain. The defects remaining are likely to be the most powerful, as well as the most cunning, therefore this hexagram offers a strategy equal to the task.

Judgement

The perseverance necessary to achieve a final break-through is envisaged as a challenge against a tyrant. Whether one is oppressed from within or without, the same laws apply i.e. confrontation without compromise. This situation ought not to be undertaken alone. If the adversary is from ones community, then the strength and support of ones direct fellowship is required for a successful consummation. Should the tyrant be concealed within ones self, then it is necessary to depend on those positive forces that have accumulated, as a result of ones continuous efforts toward the Good. These attributes are imaged as joy and strength. Only in this way can evil be displaced. When looking out, we shall also be looking in, and so in seeing the faults of others we can observe where the same defects lurk within ourselves. The benefit is twofold, in that the discredit falls always upon evil, while the practice of working for the Good is seen to be without favour. Strength and joy therefore come to mean working toward that which is without fault.

Image

Stubbornness is perceived as a blockage. When one has resolutely developed character strength to the point of a break-through, it becomes even more imperative to continue the search for the flaws, which create such an obstruction. Pride and arrogance are the self-deceptions that drive the tyrant, and these overwhelm at the time of greatest strength. Again it must be noted that, at this point, the work toward the Good ought to be done with strength that is led by joy.

The lines	*First line*

Our first efforts to remove the final obstruction are likely to be taken without knowing the power of the opposition, and a defeat is probable. If all of ones energies have been blindly used at this time, it is certain to produce a feeling of melancholy. There is the added danger of being connected with the desire of the fourth line to press forward in its own strength. The only solution is to accept the defeat and wait quietly for the positive forces to lead one back to the correct path.

Second line

This yang line is in a yin position and therefore in darkness. Fear comes because of this darkness and the reaction is to reach for a weapon. There is no wisdom in this because evil cannot be defeated with sharp swords or words, only by having no place in which it might use its own weapons. Returning to the knowledge that joy is the primary protection leads to a favourable outcome.

Third line

This line is at the core of the determination required to remove the blockage, but it has a direct link with the energies to be expelled. In the same way this line depicts the man who must directly relate to those in whom these defects are the greatest. The reason for this lies in the strength of his resolve to overcome evil no matter where it abides. The fact that he appears to be in fellowship with inferior people will lead others to shun him. He must accept this as a normal part of the work he has undertaken. It is in this way that one dispenses the energies that one has been given.

Fourth line

Stubbornness born of spiritual pride, and coupled

with self-will, is the major defect of this line. As with the first line, the humiliations that come as a result of such arrogance hopefully lead to an attitude of humility, though this is not guaranteed.

Fifth line

This is the ruler of the hexagram. Its place and energy illustrates the idea, within the attributes of the image as a whole. Joy and perseverance to overcome the obstruction and produce a break-through. The difficulties, however, are major in that it is in close proximity to the danger at all times, which threatens to wear down its resolve. The sage is released from the power of defective attitudes by his continuous efforts toward a break-through. Working tirelessly to improve the fortune of others is his protection from the self-centredness, which would destroy him.

Sixth line

The evil personified by this top line is depicted as having the capabilities of the shadow. Able to cling to, and take the shape of all things, whether of a physical or psychological nature, as well as to conceal itself in any darkness whatsoever. No matter what action is taken, the shadow is capable of moving with it, and cannot be dislodged. Only when the light is directly overhead does it die. Truth, then, and joyful movement toward this truth, is the final solution to all evil, whatever its source and wherever it is to be found.

44 Kou – Coming to meet
Heaven over wind
Fifth month – June/July
Summer solstice

The dark line has entered the hexagram, like a shadow at midday, and attempts to create an influence. The light lines must try to keep it in check, to prevent a collapse of the structure. Symbolised is the summer solstice, when the sun is no longer directly overhead and the shadows begin to appear at midday. This suggests a time when the dark force makes its first movement toward the light, and because of vanity, the strong element has welcomes it. When the danger of the situation is has been noted, it falls to the central lines in the second and fifth places to constrain its influence.

Judgement
Where a weak line attempts to hold up five strong lines, there is certain to be a collapse. When a single woman controls five men, society is threatened, for each will seek to marry her, and conflict will result. Also depicted is a situation where a subordinate has found a means to control his superiors, and must now be resisted. Other meetings are more favourable, for instance when attempting to enter a fellowship, it pays to approach its leader with humility.

Image

The heavenly influence is above, the gentle wind
carries its message to everyone, regardless of station,
and all prosper according to their nature. It is when
we try to control the message, or alter it, that it
becomes shadowy and diffused. The lines show the
various methods we can use to recognise and check
this dangerous tendency, before the darkness becomes
too great and we are overwhelmed.

The lines	*First line*

When inferior ideas first make their appearance, they
seem inviting and harmless, but when they takes hold
we observe their true nature. Here the idea has been
noticed before it becomes habitual, and its negative
influence infects the good work done upon the
character.

Second line

This is the first line of defence keeping the one below
in check, and protecting the minister in the fourth
from negative influence. The lower trigram, wind, is
gentle and so its method of control cannot be
aggressive, rather it should strike up an accord with
the dark line. In this way it is possible to preserve
even the bottom line from injury.

Third line

Always suffering the worst from temptation, this line
is protected by the wall of strength and good will
from the one below, and so the effect of the first line is
not enough to induce the third into negative traits.

Fourth line

It is the duty of the fourth line to minister to the spiritual needs of the people, but complacency has set in. The minister has character, but not enough to put others first, which means his message has become diluted. Because of this vanity his eyes are on heaven, and he cannot see the shadow of his own defects growing beneath him. Eventually they must again overwhelm him.

Fifth line

The ruling line depends entirely on the source of his strength and character, which is at the centre of his being. He is therefore unaffected by the influence of the bottom line. He is able to meet it in a natural manner with the second line, and protect it from evil consequences. This represents a time where complacency, brought about by a long period of plenty, has allowed decay to gain a foothold. Only the man of experience can respond to this correctly, for only he can recognise it as a natural situation.

Sixth line

The personality of this line reacts, rather than responds, and so cannot help those suffering in the lowest place. He is unable to take his experience back into the world and so becomes a recluse, but there is no wrong in this for he is not suited for the work.

45 Ts'ui – Gathering Together
Lake over earth

The fifth and fourth lines, representing the father and son, rule this hexagram in which the attributes of the trigrams, joy and communal interest, contribute to its meaning. A lake is a gathering of water, representing spiritual sustenance, in the world of people, from which comes the idea of re-assembling the original nature by letting go of the artificial reality.

Judgement
When people form communities they are held together by a code of morals grounded in spiritual belief. The force of this belief is to be found in their religious observances and traditions. Chinese culture translated these practices through sacrifices to the ancestors, which in term is symbolic of returning to the essential nature. A community requires a leader, and its religion functions through a minister, therefore the fourth and fifth lines are at the centre of the hexagram. The leader teaches the art of transformation, through freedom from preconceived thought patterns, while the minister teaches the function of spiritual freedom through practical experience.

Image
The lake that has no outlet can easily spill over,
swamping the surrounding areas if precautions are
not taken. When people gather together there is the
danger that excessive energies might create
unexpected problems, and so the community
practices religious observances. It is these activities
that free them from the excesses of emotions and
desires.

The lines	*First line*

When a group has no leader it has no central code of
ethics, and changing opinion controls them all. If a
leader appears, it is best to ignore the apathetic voices
and ask for his help, or the group will stagnate
through lack of direction.

	Second line

The obstacles to true fellowship and freedom from
negative thought patterns, come from our community
and the prejudicial attitudes that we share with them.
If we listen to the conscientious voice within, we will
find someone on whom we can honestly depend.

	Third line

A strong will and negative desires block the third line
from entering into a positive fellowship, but once he
has reached a condition of misery and despair he
must do so of necessity. He might feel some shame in
this, but this is a part of the change from arrogance to
humility.

Fourth line

The minister is at the centre of his community, working tirelessly to hold them together. Because he knows the true nature of their problems, he can see past the superficial and the artificial, and offer simple and practical solutions.

Fifth line

The central character influences his community through understanding and inner strength. He is neither self-opinionated nor judgemental, and so those who are unconvinced at first, seek him out at a later date. When a man has removed the blockages from his character, even those people of a mean disposition eventually ask his help.

Sixth line

The egoist is driven to seek the solution to his life's problems through strange philosophies and codes. This is because he lays too much emphasis on reason and the intellect. If he becomes willing to try another avenue he will see that the problem, and therefore the solution, is of a spiritual nature.

46 Sheng – Pushing Upward
Earth over wind, wood

The tree gradually penetrates the soil, pressing upward toward the light and life. Line five is the ruler, who pushes upward, toward heaven and enlightenment. The hexagram as a whole suggests taking positive and affirmative action, in simple steps, toward freedom from dark thought patterns that cling to the mind. The emphasis is on effort: it is symbolised by a shoot, blindly pushing through the soil toward heaven. In the same way it is necessary to enlist the help of the enlightened man, who has completed the process and is willing to act as a guide past the many traps and obstacles.

Judgement

The success of the time of pressing upward comes from making honest effort toward the good. Successful, because what we are seeking lies in the realm of the spirit, and honest because we follow the path of one who has completed the process. The pathway is slow and difficult, and is seen as rising in a series of steps, each one overcoming a different obstacle. Without the correct guide the outcome would be uncertain at best.

Image
Easy progress is symbolised by the attribute of wood, as it presses through the soil in accord with its nature, in continuous movement no matter what the obstacle. The superior man takes this as his example, as he perseveres in his efforts toward the good.

The lines
First line

The shoot pushes against the soil in its efforts to rise to the surface, symbolising the strength of will required, to make the first movement toward freedom. When we open up to our true natures, we are led by intuition to reach up to those of like mind, for assistance.

Second line

The strong character of this line corresponds with the ruler above, and follows his direction toward the goal. Taking the correct steps he achieves humility and enlightenment.

Third line

The attitude of this personality is ruled by his desires, and so the path he follows is easy and comfortable. He then assumes he has reached his goal. There is no blame attached to this, because his honest desire to accomplish what is right will eventually lead him to the proper path.

Fourth line

Through honest effort we have reached our goal. The shoot has pushed its way out of the dark soil, and we have entered the world of the spirit. We have the achieved the insight necessary to aid others on the same path, and the humility to work alongside those who went before us.

Fifth line

When the mind is empty of clutter, when it comfortably seeks the will of God it is wise to remember the dangers of complacency. Lacking conflict in the ego and instincts, we feel as though we never had a problem, were never in despair or turmoil, and it is at this moment that we can begin to judge others.

This leads backwards, so it is important to persevere with the work of restitution of our natures, and helping others to find the same path.

Sixth line

The egoist follows a path of his own design, and is unable to accept the concept of personal defeat. When difficulties arise, others are to blame; when obstacles appear, life is unfair. This condition worsens until self-pity and despair force him into a position where he must find a new attitude. If he accepts another as his guide, and follows his directions with consistency and honesty, he finds his way out of the maze.

47 K'un – Exhaustion
Lake over water

The water has drained from the lake into the abyss, which creates the idea of the light power hemmed in by darkness. All of this symbolises loss of energy and therefore exhaustion. In the structure of the hexagram as a whole light lines are hampered by dark lines, which again represents energy that cannot be used. Finally, in the attributes of the trigrams, we have the suggestion of how the sage, represented by the second and fifth lines, deals with the time of exhaustion: cheerful acceptance and constant, easy movement toward the good.

Judgement
For the sage, the time of exhaustion comes as naturally as the time of plenty, and so his actions are the same: he remains steadfast in his resolve, and continues to work cheerfully on his own character. Despite the apparent lack of spiritual energy, his confidence that hard times hold the seeds for a successful future, keeps him in harmony with the requirements of the time. For those who practice gratitude only in the good times, and collapse into self-pity and resentment when there is a drought, the time of exhaustion is a testing ground.

Image

When the waters of the lake have sunk into the depths, life on the surface suffers deprivation: drought is a natural phenomenon, and comes and goes in its time. It is the same with spiritual sustenance, symbolised by water: there are times when, because of physical exhaustion, it appears to have drained away. The superior man knows that it is hidden in the secret depths of his being, and that he must rest physically for a time, so that he can be refilled.

The lines	*First line*

When we first feel the affects of exhaustion we should examine our inner reactions, searching for negative mental and emotional responses, and deal with them immediately. But if we fall into depression at this stage, there is little chance we will escape the ravages of the deprivations to come.

Second line

Hemmed in by dark lines: there is not enough spiritual sustenance, but the sage withdraws into his deeper self in prayer, and contemplation of the meaning of the time. In this way he comes to understand the principle of increase and decrease: when things are full they begin to empty, and when empty they fill up.

Third line

This personality is driven by negative emotions from one extreme to the other: seeking satisfaction in the wrong places; creating difficulties where none existed.

Unless he can accept that his problem is lack of spiritual power, he is doomed to a life of one unnecessary defeat after another.

Fourth line

When we are recuperating, after a long period, we are tempted to proceed carefully unless we cause a relapse. This line, as the minister, is filled with an abundance of power for the benefit of those who depend on him, so it is a shameful act to withhold energy for himself. Once he has seen his mistake, however, he moves at once to their aid.

Fifth line

The ruler has inner strength and the desire to help the people, but no fellowship to work with. A spiritual leader must wait until he is approached, and so until his teaching is required he withdraws into his inner self for direction from God.

Sixth line

In times of exhaustion mistakes are made, wrong directions taken, but remorse and guilt serve only to block progress. An honest regret, a willingness to move to a better ideal dissolves these obstacles as if they never existed.

48 Ching – The Well

Water over wind/wood
The expansion of character

Wooden poles were used to draw clay buckets from the well in ancient China, and this provides the image of the distribution of basic needs among the community. When people decide to build a community, the location of water is a primary factor, and if there is no surface water they dig a well. This is the simplest of structures, just as the character of the sage-king is simple. There must be depth, and a limitless supply of water. The fifth line is the ruler, who represents the channel for unlimited spiritual nourishment, for all who require it.

Judgement

Communities, like plants, need a tap-root though which they can satisfy their most basic needs. Every society, and each individual within that society, has the potential for spiritual growth, but this depends on good leaders and teachers. The governing body needs to structure the community around these essential requirements, in such a way that everyone can take what they need. Spiritual growth is achieved when character reaches the 'water of life' deep within and the central character in a community requires this depth, to be a channel for the spiritual sustenance of those around him.

Image

Just as roots draw water from the ground to benefit
the tree, so the sage-king draws upon the divine in his
nature, to dispense to his community. A well, like the
character of a person, has worth only in as much as it
is used, and a well which sinks only half way to water
is as useless as no well at all.

The lines   *First line*

If one chooses to build his house in the swamp,
others in the community will desert him. The parallel
to this, regarding ones character, is not to dwell in
depressive areas of the mind.

Second line

This personality has all the requirements for spiritual
growth, but chooses to go fishing with no keep-net.
Seeking self-satisfaction he associates with others of
like mind. Eventually he seeks into the mud of the line
beneath.

Third line

Here also we find a personality with good character,
but though he seeks good works no-one approaches
him. This is place of the instincts, and his motives,
though good lack the required depth. The solution for
this line is to make an approach to the superior
character in the fifth place.

Fourth line

This man has made the approach, and is in the
process of self-improvement. This means that he is
not available for work, like a well that is being

repaired is not accessible, but when the alterations are finished, he will be able to achieve greater things then he could previously have imagined.

Fifth line

Here we find the central character whose nature befits the work. He is the perfect channel for the spiritual needs of people, and can be approached by all without fear or favour. Such a leader is like a well that is ignored, if there is no one to hear his words.

Sixth line

This line personifies the actions to be taken by those who follow the example of the fifth line, and reach the waters of life within themselves. Whatever one receives should be dispensed to others who need it.

49 Ko – Revolution
Lake over fire

Fire in the lake describes how selfish desires become unselfish, as a result of extreme changes. Fire and water conflict in their natures from which comes the idea of revolution, whose positive aspect is suggested by the attributes of the trigrams. Joy comes from clarity and clarity is increased by happiness. We are born with both of these qualities, but lose them as we become conditioned by the demands of ego and instinct. Habitual thinking dulls the clarity of mind; illusory satisfactions create deep unhappiness; finally we remember nothing of the original nature. The solution to this blindness comes from a deflation of the ego at depth, so that the true nature can rise again.

Judgement
Revolutions are a last resort, and they require a leader not driven by self-serving motives. To lead the people through radical changes, to a happy and enlightened existence, he must have no underlying extremes of his own. Deflating the ego, and reducing the demands of the instincts, begins with knowledge of the workings of self. With this knowledge we can move toward a full understanding of the diseased self, and a sincere decision to overthrow its governing aspects. With a

proper guide, self-knowledge comes easy, but without sincerity nothing can be accomplished.

Image

The image of the battle between fire and water has a parallel, in the constant battle between light and darkness, which produces the season of the year and the cycle of day and night. Clarity and happiness comes from our knowledge and manipulation of these changes, as it does from knowing that through internal conflict, we are restored to our original nature, and granted the power to carry out great changes.

The lines	*First line*

Without the direction of a clear-minded teacher it is foolish to begin a revolution, especially when we have no real idea of the nature of the problem. If we attempt an offensive now, we can only deal with its outward manifestations. It is better to wait for the right time and proper guidance, and we can remove it root and branch.

Second line

This personality has a sincere desire to complete the inner changes. He has tried every avenue he knows, and all that remains is a complete revolution. His compatibility with the leader in the fifth place, and willingness to make any sacrifice, suggest that this is the correct time.

Third line

When the personality demands changes, it can only imagine extremes. For some faults it leans to self-justification and for others self-loathing: either a clean sweep or no real changes at all. If the time is correct for drastic action, an honest request for help will not be refused. However, if the time is not right, then we may have to be patient and make the request three times.

Fourth line

The responsibility of the mediator is to carry the teaching of the ruling line above, but before he can do this he must go through the refining process himself. The time is correct and he is sincere in his desire for change.

Fifth line

The sage is transformed, to such an extent that his instincts and ego are directed by inner truth, and strengthened by the will of God. When people approach him for help, the guidelines he offers are clear and simple, and the results revolutionary.

Sixth line

Those with a sincere desire to change from the inside out, follow the clear guidelines of the central character, having faith that such revolutionary changes are possible. Those who have no real faith, only seek to change their appearances, believing they can improve their lives by false displays of humility. They remain selfish in their hearts, continue to abuse those who come close to them, and accuse others of the vices that control them.

50 Ting – The Cauldron
Fire over wood

When wood burns, the caldron is heated, and the
food within is refined so that the family is nourished.
The ruler is the fifth line, who is open to the teachings
of a sage in the sixth line, and becomes able to rule
with an intelligent and open mind: in this way the
people are nourished. The man of character is
enlightened, because he is receptive to the power and
will of God, and satisfies the deeper needs of those
who follow him, through his teachings. The process of
refining the will requires a sustained and determined
effort, but its outcome depends entirely on humility.

Judgement
Wood is refined through fire, and all that exists is
refined as it enters the world of the spirit. The
process, mentioned above, is symbolised by the
religious practice of offering a sacrifice to God: the
sacrifice being that of the earthly will and desires,
which are then refined in the realm of the spirit. God
speaks through sage and prophet, in whom this
fulfilment of this process can be observed as humility.

Image
The fire depends on the wood, and the caldron upon
the flame. There is no refinement without the process,

and so the superior man offers his will and life to God, so that he can become the caldron in which the change takes place, and he and others can be nourished.

The lines	*First line*

At the beginning of the process we have to get rid of the old, symbolised here by turning the pot upside down so that the scraps of food are removed. When we make ourselves empty we can be filled. This requires great courage and humility, even to start.

Second line

When we are filled with the energy and will of God, and we begin working with other people, negative forces are drawn to attack us. All that is required is continuous work toward the good, and we are protected.

Third line

The selfish desires of this personality continue to block him from working with others. When the refining process is almost finished, it is as if this man turns back and refuses to share what he has received with others. If he can to see his self-centredness, he will reject it and the process will carry through. If not, his original sacrifices will have been in vain.

Fourth line

The minister has a great responsibility, but if like the third line he practices only half measures, he will lose everything he has gained. When that happens, only inferior people seek him out and then only to use him.

Fifth line

When we have become receptive to others, with an attitude of humility that comes from persistent self-examination, they approach with a willingness to aid in the work of fellowship. To lead, a man must know how to serve, but he should also have a teacher or his ego overtakes him.

Sixth line

The teacher of the central character in the line below, is a sage who has been transformed by the work. The ultimate achievement of his efforts is a oneness with the will of God: desire and ego no longer control him, and so the world has no power over him. His teachings are spontaneous and clear, because they are not based on knowledge and opinion.

51 Chen – Thunder

Thunder over thunder
Thunder is the power to animate.
Shock

Thunder repeated: yang- virile energy, bursts from out of the earth to create an awakening. In nature this represents spring. The bottom line rules the hexagram and represents the eldest son: this is the Logos. This is how the character is refined through right and clear action: by energetically removing old habits at the moment they become evident in our daily lives. From stillness comes sudden action, and if this action is clear and well motivated others are positively influenced. This image is suggested by the nuclear trigrams, mountain (quietness within) and fire (clarity).

Judgement

Thunder is the voice of God as expressed in nature. This is also true in the nature of mankind. Fear results from the power of thunder, but when it is realised that this is the proper fear of God, it follows that other fears are only a manifestation of this. This is the way, therefore, to reverence of God and peace at the centre of being. There is a sacrifice to be made, as demonstrated by the lines. Each expresses a stage of the inner journey and the nature of the difficulties encountered there.

Image

What is imaged here is the power, which awakens in the hearts of people, whose expression we at first call fear and later, after recognising its source and purpose, we call reverence. Thunder repeated symbolises a mind so full of fears, that every attempt to get free from one area of distress, brings anxiety somewhere else. The practice of self-examination and the removal of even the slightest defect allows for a steady expansion in ones point of view.

The lines   *First line*

At the time of the first recognition of the inner voice of God, the reaction is one of fear. Fear that one is somehow different. As fear always translates negatively, this difference is perceived as a handicap, something to be hidden, but in the end when the trial is over, is recognised as strength.

Second line

This line depicts the realm of values and decisions. In real terms we suffer the shock of being disconnected from outer possessions. It is the acceptance of this sacrifice, which alters the point of view concerning property. The text suggests that the belongings, which have been lost, will be returned after seven days, meaning a full round of experience.

Third line

What is reflected within this line is a situation where our reaction to destiny is shocked immobility. The impetus to resolution must come from the shock itself. If we recognise in the thoughts that this shock is to the inner voice of God, then the ideas can take a positive direction.

Fourth line

Here the thoughts are crippled by apathy. To endure the situation while looking to the fifth line for strength- this is the only course to take. Inferior ideas can only be overcome by relating to, and therefore returning to, one's sense of Good Purpose. This is provided through the example of the line above.

Fifth line

This line shows the centre of the true Self, around which chaos reigns- the walls of the inner Kingdom battered continuously by repeated shocks. The centre is the place of neutrality: the realm of the spirit. Old habits continuously, though blindly, batter against the doors of consciousness: defence is unnecessary for their power is spent. What is required is that one's reliance remains with the inner directive and the primary design therein.

Sixth line

When shock is at its most extreme, as with the affects from a sudden explosion of force, the human system begins to shut down. At this time withdrawal into the centre, until the anxiety diminishes, is the only recourse. Others will react through their instincts only, becoming troubled at the lack of alarm, but this is the correct way of avoiding injury to the inner being. Be steadfast.

52 Chen – Mountain

Mountain over mountain
A doubled trigram
The youngest son
Stillness

The yin lines provide the foundation for the yang line,
which has reached its highest point and can go no
further. This gives the idea of rest, meaning that both
powers have found their proper place and function.
Nevertheless the book counsels that rest does not
mean inaction, rather it is a state of stillness in which
one contemplates the spiritual centre within.

Judgement

The sage contemplates the wealth within, i.e. of the
spirit, and then contemplates the manner in which it
can best be used to benefit his outer world. His view
of this outer world is expansive as a result of his
practice of the meditative exercise, in which the
limited ideas of the personality are quieted.

Image

The mountain range is the symbol of stability, in an
earthly sense. Man is of the world and should
recognise this and be steadfast in his daily duties. In
his quiet time, when the demands of life have
retreated, he should meditate on that place where his
goodness reigns- the place at the centre. Only here
can he differentiate between the true and the false.

The lines   *First line*

The humility of this line protects it from impatient action, and it waits quietly for correct support before taking any action. Correct support means finding a proper teacher.

Second line

This line has correctness born of its central position, and is able to keep still. It is unhappy because it wishes to join with a strong line, but the fifth line is weak while the third line, which is strong, is too impatient. This describes the loneliness of acting correctly.

Third line

The impatience of the instinctive man makes him inflexible at times when flexibility is required and weak when strength is demanded by the time. This places him in a position of continuous danger. Being still, despite the impulse to move, is the only protection.

Fourth line

To make a stand despite weaknesses implies a brave heart, and this personality will eventually find the inner strength required if he continues to practice self-restraint.

Fifth line

The fifth line has weaknesses that it recognises, but continues working for the benefit of others in the only way possible, which is through teaching.

Sixth line

The character of the top line contains all of the inner

wealth, as well as an expansive viewpoint. He is the sage king and is seen as resting in the ultimate good of heaven.

53 Chein – Gradual Development
Wind over mountain

Wind moving gently about the roof of the mountain is like the spirit gradually changing the conditioning created by the ego: the habitual thinking of a lifetime cannot be transformed in a moment. When the nature has awakened through the power of the spirit, we might feel that there is little left to do, but in fact the work has only just begun. Slow and gradual movement toward the good, and a willingness to make efforts in all of our daily affairs, creates a successful lifestyle that leads to wisdom.

Judgement
This hexagram counsels against an impatient attitude toward alterations in the personality, whether these are destructive habits in others or ourselves. Delusory attitudes and extreme reactions are more easily removed when we are objective about their manifestations. This attitude is depicted in the attributes of the trigrams: inner calm and conscious flexibility. The rulers, in the second and fifth places, progress carefully through many changes to secure their true natures. The fifth line represents the sage who has followed the true path, not diverted by desire for personal gain or distinction, thorough in his examination of self. This is the way to a meaningful

life.

Image

Gentle influence, the attribute of wind, is also
represented by wood, so that the meaning of the
hexagram is also imaged as a tree on the mountain.
The mountain has a strong base, and the tree grows
slowly and carefully: again we see the image of
gradual improvement. Character development comes
from the removal of the unreal in favour of the real,
from the wisdom to differentiate between the two and
the eventual translation of this process into all of our
affairs.

The lines	*First line*

The first movements toward character development
appear as failures, because of our impulsive reactions.
When we observe a defect in ourselves, we are
impatient for it to be gone, becoming irritated and
despondent when this does not happen immediately.
We should recognise these reactions as further
manifestations of the same problem, and move
toward their elimination.

Second line

As we sense the positive changes in ourselves,
recognising that these have come about as a direct
result of the process of development we have
undertaken, we experience a certain amount of
exhilaration and a desire to share our good fortune
with others. This is one of the most positive aspects of

character development.

Third line

Instinctive behaviour is the most difficult to control, especially if we have been habitually excessive in our old lives. The solution to this kind of extreme conduct lies in the surrender of judgmental opinions, and the acceptance of the need for a new attitude.

Fourth line

The minister is required to be flexible in his outlook, but his message must have a solid foundation. The practice of quiet meditation helps him to find a neutral attitude, towards the defects of himself and of others.

Fifth line

The path to unity between body and spirit, instinct and intuition, whose outcome is a full and balanced character, is blocked by many dilemmas. These restrictive attitudes continue to plague even the most sincere practitioners of character development, but in the end all false attitudes melt away.

Sixth line

When spiritual progress has reached its peak, it is time to rest and contemplate the best manner in which the process can be passed on. When this too has been fulfilled, the cycle of gradual progress can be seen as one movement.

54 Kuei mei – The Marrying Maiden
Thunder over lake
The cycle of life

From the point of view of social behaviour, we have
two interpretations of this hexagram. The first, from
patriarchal times, is where a young girl happily
follows an older man into marriage. In this case,
because of the morals of the time, the girl was at fault
in making the approach without invitation. In the
second example, from a matriarchal era, it is the girl's
brother who leads her to find a husband. The main
issue is that the individual trigrams depict the
relationship between the sexes, and also, the
hexagram as a whole symbolises the relationships
between heaven and earth and the cycle of life.

Judgement
Again, from the point of view of social order, we are
given the example of a culture in which a man is
encouraged to have more than one wife. The young
girl enters the marriage because of affection for the
man, whereas the first wife entered through contract.
What is observed in the energy of the lines, is that the
rules for social order must be dealt with in a different
way to those relationships founded on emotional
attachment. Despite the necessity for the first, society
being based on order, it is the spontaneity in
relationships that exemplifies the nature of unity. This

union, as applied to heaven and earth, results in the cycle of the seasons, through which life passes through end and beginning. When applied to the young girl, it depicts the end of her maidenhood and beginning of motherhood. Finally, in regard to the formulation of character, the hexagram shows the breadth of vision that comes from contemplating the laws indicated, by the movement of thunder. In spring it rises from the lake, returning to rest at the beginning of winter. Through contemplating only this, we can know the nature of eternity.

Image
Thunder over the lake represents the great life-giving energy, in autumn, when it is about to sink back into the earth through the waters of the lake. The lake welcomes it with enthusiasm so that the cycle of life, and cosmic order, can be fulfilled. The sage, in observing the natural order of this, is able to predict future events.

The lines	*First line*

The young girl is pictured entering the family of a prince, where because of her acceptance of her position, the wife welcomes her. Also represented is the official of the lowest rank, whose only relationship with the ruling fifth line is through a friendship with the second line. This is favourable, in that his achievements are humble despite his handicap, which is depicted as lameness.

Second line

This line is strong enough to continue to behave
correctly, although its partner in the fifth place is
weak. Like a wife whose husband no longer supports
her, this line must depend on itself for energy, though
this is a lonely path.

Third line

This line is driven by misdirected instincts, and seeks
to satisfy them at a great cost to its dignity. Like the
line at the top it lacks true direction. There is no
judgement given regarding such a situation, only the
example of its lack of self-worth.

Fourth line

This line behaves in an entirely opposite way to the
one below. It is not pressed by desires, rather it
pursues the very dignity that the third line has lost.
The marriage that it seeks in not in sight, but in time
all will change and its patience will be rewarded.

Fifth line

It is in the nature of this line to abide in its place while
others approach it.

In the present circumstances, however, it must
leave its position, despite the lack of energy (a yin line
in a strong place), and seek out its partner. The yang
line in the second place awaits its decision, if there is a
movement then the hexagram will achieve some
balance. In terms of character growth, this suggests a
real sacrifice of vanity.

Sixth line

The sacrifice depicted in this line is false, for like the

third line it is driven by selfish motivations, in this case the superficial outlook of the ego.

55 Feng – Abundance
Thunder over fire
Broadcasting spiritual principles

Thunder, the voice of God and the eldest son, draws lightning behind it, so that proclamations are made clear. The yielding fifth line is the ruler of the hexagram, who, like the midday sun, commands the central position, and distributes wealth and punishments to all. Pictured also is the comet, journeying over the heavens for a brief period, the herald of prosperous times to come. Like the passing of the comet, the time of prosperity is temporary. This shows the nature of the movement of the primary forces, which at the moment of fullness move toward emptiness.

Judgement
The sage, the fifth line, views the time of abundance with gladness, (nuclear trigram, lake) knowing that it is a time where the influence (nuclear trigram, wind) of heaven is at its greatest. Socially, there is great prosperity, but more importantly the people are clear about the rights of all in their community. This perfection can only endure, however, if the influence of spiritual principles is extended, to those not of ones direct fellowship. Failure to do this leads to stagnation and collapse. It is the responsibility of the central character, whose inner purpose prepares him

for leadership at such times, to make this clear.

Image

The image of a storm, which removes tension from the air, depicts the clarity and the swiftness of penalties to be carried out. What is significant in this image, is the necessity that justice is clearly (fire), based on the word of God (thunder), whose influence must be extended to all. This expansion of spiritual principles, into all the avenues of experience, ensures the durability of the time of prosperity. This symbolises the time when spiritual strength and intelligence working together in a productive manner.

The lines	*First line*

Encountering someone whose attributes complement ones own, is a once in a life time occurrence. For this line and the minister in the fourth place this happy circumstance has occurred, and so their brief partnership can accomplish something great. Their time together is limited, however, and both must be willing to accept the eventual separation.

Second line

The separation for this line has already taken place, between it and the ruler in the fifth place. If it clings, in the nature of flame, to the truth all goes well for it and the companion above.

Third line

The light, or influence, of this line is overshadowed, and so no action can be taken. The image is of rain clouds, which block off the sun and make its light ineffective.

Fourth line

This line is partially shadowed, but the first line travels up to meet it and their union strengthens the resolve of both. Wisdom and clarity of mind thus work together for the benefit of the ruler, above.

Fifth line

The ruler draws on the integrity of the second line and the attributes of the other lines, to increase his influence in the time of plenty. In this way great societies are formed.

Sixth line

The personality depicted in this line becomes isolated, because of his lack of humility. His spiritual strength is at first so great, that he rises above all of his difficulties, but then fails to see that is only to prepare him for the responsibility of forming a fellowship, based on the principles which elevated him. His ideas stagnate and lead him further and further from the protection of the group.

56 Lu – The Wanderer

Fire on the mountain

It is said that a man cannot be a prophet in his own town, and so it fits his nature that such a person becomes a wanderer. Fire on the mountain exists only where there is fuel, just as the wanderer lingers only where he can be of use, and so when his work is finished he vanishes like the flame. When we enter a place as a stranger, if we are to have any influence whatsoever our behaviour should project humility. If we have a message it ought to be delivered as if those who choose to contact us already knew it. The fifth line rules the hexagram and exemplifies the kind of conduct demanded by the time of the wanderer.

Judgement

The ruling line is yin, and therefore has humility as its attribute. It is able to behave with respect to those who rule in each community, while observing with complete clarity. It is this clarity, born of steadfastness, which is the main protection against involvement with dangerous forces.

Image

The flame seen on a mountain is like that of the shooting star, it is momentary and quickly forgotten. The hexagram suggests that this is the way to deal

with trespass and other minor infringements.
Penalties should be immediate and then forgotten.
True justice is not served by long resentful actions.

The lines   *First line*

The first line depicts ones opening movements, on
which we are judged, and suggests a dignified rather
than demeaning approach. Whether we attempt to
seek friendship through arrogance or foolish
behaviour, the result is the same: rejection and
contempt. This is because we are projecting a false
nature.

Second line

This personality has much character, without the
defects of the lower line, which is willing to act as a
follower. In such a way are great fellowships formed.

Third line

The instinctive personality tends to leap to opposite
extremes in his dealings with people, and so drive
away those who would welcome and those who
seeking to follow him. He is like the fire that swiftly
consumes everything in a small area then dies out.

Fourth line

The minister has learned how to control his
instinctive behaviour, and so finds friends and a place
of his own in a strange community. Inside of himself
he recognises that he does not belong, and so finds no
comfort. This is the wanderer's fate- always to be a
stranger.

Fifth line

This line also makes friends, but does so by being of use to those above and below, which is a true act of humility. He accepts only what is due to him, and only what is useful. When we are not in competition for resources, yet willing to offer all that we have, people accept us gladly.

Sixth line

The ego of this line is so great that it believes it can behave in any way that it wishes, now that it has been accepted in the community. It has gone too far and cannot see that it is isolated and in danger.

57 Sun – Gentleness
Wind over wind
Suggests homecoming
The measure of character

The primary meaning of this hexagram lies in the nature of the movement of both wind and wood. A tree sends its roots into the dark earth, slowly and gently, seeking the path of least resistance. Wind fills the space between sky and soil scattering storm clouds. The character, personified by these gentle movements, is one who is able to find and examine the shadowy motivations that masquerade as truth, both in himself and elsewhere. This he can do because of the gentle aspect of his nature, which exposes hidden faults without condemnation.

Judgement
The energy required to produce sudden and remarkable changes in the personality is called by many names, one of which is a spiritual experience. This form of effect might be depicted in 22 Grace, but the influence depicted here is more constant and therefore its effects travel further. In the former, it is more the individual who receives, but in this hexagram the entire community is affected. At the centre of society, as in the centre of the individual, there needs to be a neutral character capable of inducing small, but positive movements toward the Good.

Image

The hexagram is made up of wind leading wind, therefore an enduring but gentle influence. The blockages to character growth are removed by the first wind while the energy to act correctly comes from the second. As a result one gains a conscious understanding of the will of the Good, while receiving the energy to carry it out.

The lines	*First line*

In ones first attempts at the kind of changes required for inner worth, one is naturally assailed by doubts. Here a fundamental discipline, as dictated by those in the line above, is essential. Doubt and fear are the first blocks to growth. Once one has recognised this, they have no power.

Second line

This line advises the employment of mediators in examining those areas where the motives are destructive, yet difficult to shake loose. Sometimes these influences are indistinct and can only be identified by their nature, but because of their subtlety they cannot pin down. Here the book suggests the employment of experts, in order to follow their influences to their source. Priests and magicians serve as the mediators between the hidden realm and that of the seen, though it may be worth noting that some modern psychologists have taken over their function in modern society.

Third line

The Art of War, by Sun Tsu counsels that drawn-out strategies only serve to deplete ones energies. Line three suggests the same idea. When the nature of the difficulty has been noted, it is time to seek help in its removal. This line attempts too much on its own power, and there is no forward motion.

Fourth line

This line lacks the energy to press on alone, but as it has much experience and is at the place of the mediator it calls the three bottom lines to join it. All can move on in safety and strength, having formed a fellowship based on spiritual growth.

Fifth line

Again it is worth referring to 'The art of war' regarding the actions required by this line. Before any confrontation one must first make calculations regarding costs, and when the end is reached, further calculations are needed to assess the viability of the actions taken. The line is in the centre of the upper trigram, and therefore is the ruler of the hexagram. Holding the place of centre is fraught with great dangers and great responsibility, for even when the goal is in sight this line is not allowed to rest. Every end includes a new beginning and the preparations must again be made.

Sixth line

This line denotes a time when the energies are so depleted that to continue forward would bring danger. The only solution is to turn around and join the line below with which it is connected. This suggestion signifies the homecoming in the opening lines. There is a parallel here in the biblical story of the prodigal son.

58 Tui – The Joyous Lake

Lake over lake
Joy is the nature of reality
When people are joyous they strengthen each other
A doubled trigram

The hexagram of joy repeated represents a time when
the people have achieved strength within, and express
this outwardly in happiness. In terms of character
development, it depicts the joy of working with
others. The lake holds water, the most basic need of
the community. This also symbolises vital energy, and
a community obedient to spiritual principles. The
second and fifth lines are the rulers because of their
strength and position, whereas the top lines of each
trigram define the gentleness with which the energy is
manifest.

Judgement

When joy is shared through a gentle attitude, others
are grateful to participate in ones fellowship. This is
because they are attracted to the kind of work which
satisfies their deepest needs. At the centre of everyone
is the desire for wholeness, and the greatest part of
this comes from strengthening others. The power of
joy is strong enough to overcome all human fears.
When certain elements in a community observe a
strength, which is not used to control others, they are
led to test it. This kind of testing has only one
purpose: to pollute and degrade the nature of

character.

Image

Two lakes, the image of a spiritual community. As one empties, the other is there to fill it up again. It is the same with groups who share intuitive knowledge, and the practical applications of what they have learned. They seek out new combinations and uses, and always with a happy heart.

The lines	*First line*

Strength and humility are the primary attributes of gratitude. Resting in the knowledge that we has been freed, if only for a moment, from former prejudices, we come to an understanding of the Divine will.

Second line

The thoughts of this line are constantly provoked by the desires of the line above, but it is in the central place and is not tempted. To make this an enduring condition means a determined approach to the other strong line in the fifth place. Distracted thoughts strengthen the central purpose, which is to work toward the Good.

Third line

Joy comes via the heart, but a heart enmeshed in self-satisfaction has only an increasing desire, and therefore an increasing frustration. This is because instincts overwhelm the hearts true desire, perceived as Oneness with man and God.

Fourth line

The fourth line is the place of the mediator, a difficult and dangerous position, should we allow desires to seduce us into lowering our hard won principles. The fifth line is strong and draws us up, and we move accordingly. It would be foolish and dangerous to look backwards with nostalgia.

Fifth line

This line has great strength for itself and those who look up to it, but if it should offer fellowship to the arrogant sixth line it would lose its correctness. The situation depicts how the sage must deal with the great joy that comes to him, as a result of the cultivation of character. If it is shared with others, all goes well, but if not, he is easily tempted to use it for his own pleasure.

Sixth line

Here is the situation hanging over the head of the ruling line. Once a man has achieved something great, if he is not aware of the dangers, vanity can sweep him away and all that he has worked for is lost. The only solution is to work vigorously toward the Good.

59 Huan – Dispersion
Wind over water

When water, representing spiritual energy, is frozen or dammed up so that it cannot be utilised, the gentleness and warmth of wind can disperse it into cloud and carry it off. The ruler is the yang fifth line whose duty it is to remove the blockages to harmony in the world. Correspondence and support comes from the strong second line, while the devoted minister in the fourth place carries out the distribution of his work.

Judgement

The second, fourth and fifth lines work in conjunction, to achieve dispersion of the energy that has been obstructed. This is how the superior character draws on all of his energies to improve his character. 'The king approaches his temple while his servant waits below. A strong character comes, and receives abundant energy from above.' The symbolism here directly parallels that of the Holy Trinity: the fifth line being the Father, the second the Son and the fourth line represents the Holy Spirit. The obstructions, which they disperse, represent those defective attitudes, which manifest as blocks to the unity of man. The Great Work at such times was accomplished in two ways. The first was through religious celebration, where the hearts of all were awakened to the unity of mankind through God, and the second by way of working toward the good, through a common need. With regards to the work of the sage-king, this hexagram marks a new beginning, or an awakening of new energy. The character at the centre of such a task would need to be free of all selfish ties, therefore free to follow his duty

Image

In spring the air is warm and dissolves the rigidity of winter. In the same way that men's hearts, hardened by prejudice, can be softened by a religious experience. This awakening of the spirit means they can know fellowship with God and man.

The lines   First line

This line represents a new and willing member of a fellowship, who depends on the more experienced character in the line above, for direction and strength. This dependency is necessary at the beginning, to prevent errors due to misunderstanding, and to help in the healing of old wounds.

Second line

Recognising the destructive nature of his prejudices, this personality achieves salvation by reaching out to the central line in the fifth place. What is implied is a return to clarity and good will, after a period of time where such a view was obstructed by self-serving motives. The energy that returns to him is inexhaustible, just as the field of his influence is ever widening.

Third line

It is the nature of the instincts to protect the self, but when these desires obstruct the expansion of the character it is necessary to disperse their influence. The top line of the upper trigram aids this act of humility and the dangers of self-will are averted.

Fourth line

Even the bonds of friendship can be a block to the will of God, and so these also must now be dissolved. Such an act, to forego the ties to ones group (the three bottom lines), requires courage, and this can only come from a stronger connection to the central character in the line above. The purpose of this step is to achieve an attitude not available to the self. The group does not suffer as a result of this, for the second line has taken its place as leader.

Fifth line

'The king has reached his temple and his will spreads to the farthest corners of his kingdom'. In the central place a man of his time, inspired at the moment of greatest defeat by a single idea: an idea of such depth and weight that it awakens the enthusiasm of everyone who hears it. The fourth line directly supports him by expanding into fellowship and the second line by carrying the simple message.

Sixth line

This line exemplifies the nature of the message. That the way to avoid danger, is to help others to avoid it.

60 Chieh – Limitation

Water over lake
Freedom of choice means accepting ones nature

Rain falls and fills the lake to its limits. Should this
continue there would be a flood, therefore the
hexagram shows limitation as a necessary condition
of life. A society that practices economy prepares itself
for difficult times. The sage designs a code of morals
bounded by duty and detachment. The strong line in
the fifth place, whose purpose it is to create the best
example for the other lines, practises this attitude.

Judgement
Living to excess today creates deficiency tomorrow,
and for this reason the practice of limiting desires is
paramount. It is equally important not to be excessive
in restricting such powerful forces, or we invite a
backlash. An over-indulgence of one instinct tempts a
flood of reactions from other appetites, just as in
society, the temptation to place restrictions on others,
is the cause of most conflicts. The ruler of the
hexagram examines his own character for defects,
while observing the strengths in others.

Image
Water fills up empty spaces: the lake is an example of
this. This represents the man of simple means, willing
to dispense all that he possesses because he knows

that, like the lake, he will be replenished in time. Nevertheless, he cannot waste himself on useless projects, for he is limited in terms of time.

The lines   *First line*

If one is to avoid dangerous conflicts, it pays to stand in a place of safety. Only when ones understanding and resources appear equal to the situation, will it be time to make an assault.

Second line

The lake is filled and about to burst its banks. The time for planning is over- ones forces are assembled and ready for battle.

Third line

Because this line is involved in satisfying excessive desires, the moment for action passes, and the temptation is to blame others for the blindness, but there is no advantage in this. Only when we accept the true nature of the problem can we move toward its dismissal.

Fourth line

This line rests within the limits of its own nature. As a yin line it receives and passes on the energies, which flow toward it from the line above. This means all its actions are natural and from the centre, and for the benefit of all.

Fifth line

The example of the ruler is to limit his own desires, while distributing all of his wealth to others. If he were to amass wealth of whatever nature for himself, and limit the desires of others, he would encounter resistance. Because his character has no dependencies, he cannot be drawn from his primary purpose, and because he is centred, his movements are simple. This attitude is easy to emulate, and so others follow him.

Sixth line

Excessive restrictions excite extreme reactions. When the people are oppressed, they think of revolution and when instincts are denied, they eventually suffer a violent outburst. Despite the idea that an excess of limitations ought to be avoided, situations occur that call for rigorous action. Usually when ones spiritual development is threatened by character defects. At these times only vigorous effort toward the good prevents a collapse.

61 Chung fu – Inner Truth

Wind over lake
One can depend on inner truth

At the centre of the hexagram as a whole there is an empty space, representing a humble heart: the third and fourth lines are yin, meaning they are ready to receive. The central lines of the individual trigrams are yang, and stand in place of the sincerity of content, and so their attributes represent the gentle spirit of truth, and the pleasure that comes from knowing ones true nature. The yin lines make themselves vulnerable to the yang lines, and so each attains its nature within the hexagram. This structure personifies the simplicity of inner truth.

Judgement

Because the central lines of the trigrams are yang, trust is certain, and so the yin lines representing the heart, willingly open up to their influence. In the same manner, we open up to inner truth at the moment that we let go of our dependence on old prejudices. Arrogance and intolerance serve only to shield us from the responsibility that comes from seeing, clearly, the truth in any situation. The hexagram depicts, for the man who would influence those people whose natural energies are blocked, the manner in which they ought to be approached. Only an open-minded attitude, free of all prejudice, can break through the wall built by the defensive will, but once done such a bond cannot be broken, because it is moulded from inner truth.

Image

Wind lifts water from the lake, and the words of the superior man stirs the hearts of men to experience truth. From insight comes understanding and understanding produces insight. True justice cannot exist without these primary attributes.

The lines
First line

To be free to experience the gifts that come with an open mind, it is necessary to give up our dependence on the opinions of others.

Second line

As we become accustomed to the force of insight, the barriers between us are removed. This is the true bond between human beings, which transcends time and distance, and is dependent only on honest sentiment.

Third line

As this line represents our instinctive relationships with other people, it depicts the condition of a life, which cannot depend on inner truth. Being pressed from one extreme to another, from happiness to misery and back again without reconciliation is the fate of the person governed by emotions.

Fourth line

The fourth line is the minister, whose duty it is to

carry the true message of the ruler in the fifth line and follow his directions. To do this means giving up prejudicial alliances.

Fifth line

A fellowship requires a strong character at its centre, whose will is based on the force of inner truth, or the fellowship eventually collapses under the weight of conflicting opinions.

Sixth line

At the top of the trigram of wind, this personality has no direct connection with the spiritual force in the lower trigram. Therefore his words come from an inflated ego and are not to be heeded.

62 Hsiao kuo – Preponderance of the Small

Thunder over mountain
Modest changes

Thunder on the mountain presents the voice of God
in a high, yet distant place. While others might feel
safe when the storm is far off, the sage recognises a
time for preparation, for small adjustments, and so he
allows his influence to be felt in common things. The
second and fifth lines, (both yielding, which suggests
a humble attitude), are the rulers of the hexagram

Judgement

The message symbolised by the upper trigram,
Thunder, is carried from the mountain, but it ought to
be remembered here that we are the messenger only
and not the message. No one is prepared to listen to
the voice of arrogance, preaching from a spiritual
hilltop. The requirements are an excess of caution and
humility and careful observation of the situation at
hand.

Image

In stillness, i.e. meditation, the sage listens to the
distant voice of God and acts accordingly. What is
suggested by this image, is that there are times when
the man of character is compelled to deal directly
with minor problems that arise in the course of the
day. Thus he is seen to be a man with a man's
difficulties and therefore approachable. Though

others might perceive his actions to be trivial, still it is required that he follows his nature, which is to duty.

The lines   *First line*

This line is at the base of the mountain and should be still, but seeks fellowship with the strong nine in the fourth place, and so moves without the required caution. This is extremely dangerous.

Second line

This yin line corresponds with the fifth, and is depicted as following in the path of her grandmother. As the nature of the ruling line above is presented as eminently modest, so also is this line.

Third line

The arrogance of the self-sufficient man is on the one hand offensive and on the other a beacon for evil elements. Those who would support him are driven away by his attitude, so that no one protects his back from unseen dangers.

Fourth line

The minister has humility of his own, so that the energy of this line does not press him into danger. An excess of caution is required.

Fifth line

The yin line does not have the power to create spiritual changes because its energy is that of the world. It is necessary to search for a leader whose work is known to be correct, and join with him. As the work is of a spiritual nature, a further explanation might be to seek the entity within ones own character, but this must be accomplished with humility.

Sixth line

Because this personality is egocentric he refuses to join the quiet group below. His attitude demands personal recognition and so he goes off alone. Like the third line, he attracts only inferior people who will eventually subvert him.

63 Chi chi – After Completion
Water over fire

This hexagram represents the peak of attainment: the individual lines are all in their proper places, and everything moves according to its shih, meaning its correct time. The image of perfect achievement represents a condition, where time and place are right for harmonious transformation. It is a time of balance and social order, at the pinnacle of human accomplish-ment. But this fact, that success has reached its ultimate position, indicates that the process of evolving is about to enter a period of decline. The second line rules the hexagram, because at the beginning of change there is stability: while things are balanced we can prepare for the period of danger ahead. The fifth line, which is usually the place of the ruler, is at the end of the period of development when confusion has entered the picture, and so depends on the support of the second line.

Judgement
When situations are at the climax of development, they begin to alter, to move in the opposite direction. This is the law of change: the waxing and waning of yin and yang, light and dark- expansion presupposing contraction. For the period of completion to be maintained then, it is necessary to prevent total fulfilment of the change. The superior man attempts

to do this by including elements opposed to all out transformation. By his awareness of the possibility of danger, of destruction and chaos, he retains temporal ideas and attitudes, which prevent the culmination of spirit and vital energy.

Image

Water cools fire, fire heats water- together these elements balance each other. Fire represents spirit, while water represents the vital energy. When the spirit directs the energy and the energy fulfils the work of the spirit, then habitual thinking loses power, but if there is an accumulation of either, there creates an imbalance, which manifests as irritation and restlessness. In knowing that the true nature of this condition is of the spirit, the man of character prevents a decline into apathy and rebellion.

The lines	First line

The danger at the beginning of prosperity is that we can become drunk with success, along with everybody else. Having reached the goal after a long period of effort, it is wise to prevent collapse by a quiet awareness of the danger.

	Second line

Those who have achieved success and power are often blinded, by their own self-importance, and feel no need for further guidance. Having found a degree of comfort, they slip into a condition of complacency, from which they may not awaken. Though the central character foresees this, he may not intervene, until such times as they recognise their own danger.

Third line

At a time when inner worth is at a climax, it is unwise to allow inferior energies to control our lives. Though we may have cast out many of our old habits, instincts can always find new ways to infiltrate our lives, and so we need to watch for their manifestations.

Fourth line

When culture is at its height, intellect seeks to impose its view on everything, but culture is an expression of the spiritual growth of a society, and as such is always in danger from the opposing forces. Ignoring the clamour, we should be aware of the small evils that hide behind the voice of vanity.

Fifth line

Sacrifice is the greatest part of religious life, but in times of plenty the sacrifices take the form of grandiosity, rather than self-sacrificing acts of humility. Simple offerings come from a repentant heart, magnificent displays from the ego. The character of this line is strong and so is aware of the dangers, but his warning is ignored.

Sixth line

After consistent effort to remove the power of the ego and instincts, we have reached the pinnacle of character expansion. If at this time we turn back to view our work, congratulating ourselves on a job well done, it is as if all our exertions have been wasted, and the ego again takes command.

64 Wei chi – Before Completion
Flame over Water

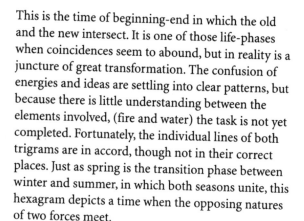

This is the time of beginning-end in which the old and the new intersect. It is one of those life-phases when coincidences seem to abound, but in reality is a juncture of great transformation. The confusion of energies and ideas are settling into clear patterns, but because there is little understanding between the elements involved, (fire and water) the task is not yet completed. Fortunately, the individual lines of both trigrams are in accord, though not in their correct places. Just as spring is the transition phase between winter and summer, in which both seasons unite, this hexagram depicts a time when the opposing natures of two forces meet.

Judgement
The responsibility appears to be overwhelming and the task itself, impossible. How can such powerful and opposing forces be reconciled? The solution lies in observing the nature of the problem, and practising caution at all times. This state of constant alertness implies that one has already learned from similar experiences and is aware of the nature of dangers. When crossing spring ice, the old fox uses all his senses to seek out the safe path, but a young fox, being inexperienced, is likely to behave with less caution and wet his tale.

Image

In any strategy correct calculations are needed to form a realistic plan. Knowing the nature of the problem requires an investigation of the nature of all of the elements involved. The energy of fire rises, while the nature of water is to press into the lowest regions. The solution lies, not in attempting to alter the nature of things but in realigning the forces so that they become related. Finally, it is necessary that ones own character be balanced, in the manner outlined above, for if not, our understanding of the problem will be biased by our own extremes.

The lines   *First line*

This line is like the young fox in the example. In attempting to rush ahead and finish the task, without making the correct calculations, failure comes as a matter of course, as does humiliation. To avoid this outcome it is necessary to practise patience.

                                         Second line

Again hesitation is suggested, for the line has more strength than is required for the place, and is inclined to immediate action. While it is not possible to go forward at this stage, if one keeps contact with the personality of the fifth line, meaning ones higher purpose, all goes well in time.

                                         Third line

This line has too little power for the necessary change therefore you must seek help from a fellowship of likeminded people. This admission of personal powerlessness is a true act of humility and is therefore the key required to complete the transition.

Fourth line

This line occupies the place of the mediator, the warrior priest, and designates the action that must now be taken to avoid complete collapse. He must lead all those who will take part in the battle with the Devil's Country, out of fear and doubt and into unquestioning faith in the eventual outcome.

Fifth line

The six in this line epitomises the nature of yin, which is devotion to the powers of light. The energy of this line, plus that of the second line, which has supported it, radiate outward, triumphantly. This is the sage character, who becomes balanced and complete, when all negative ideas and reactions have been abandoned. This is the direct result of persevering through conditions, which often seemed insurmountable.

Sixth line

This is the last line in the book of changes and reflects the full nature of change, where the beginning of what is new is to be found in the remnants of the old. The significance of this fact in terms of correct action is that it remains necessary, even when the victory is in sight, to remember ones roots. There are those who, because of their station, may rejoice and welcome the new season in an unrestrained manner, but it is essential for the sage-king to persist always in a vigilant and sober fashion in order that the new cycle of change begins favourably.

The idea, of being out of control due to drinking alcohol, is expressed in this hexagram as a great danger because; 'The sage-king loses truth, for he knows no moderation'. Alcohol and sage-dom do not mix, it seems.

Laotse (about 360BC) and Chuang-Tzu (about 340BC) are credited as the principal authors of Taoist belief.

The book known as the *Tao Te Ching*, which translates as 'The Tao and its Power', was written by Laotse and is the basic text of Taoist philosophy. Not easy to understand, this short book contains much that is paradoxical and contradictory, but the purpose of this is similar to that of the I Ching, which is to transcend rational thinking.

Chuang Tzu wrote:
When the game has been shot we can store the bow away.

Meaning that philosophy is like the key to the door, no longer required once we have passed through.

The Tao means the Way, or the Path of power. When things follow the Path assigned to them they are in accord with this power, and therefore with their nature. It was the purpose of Taoist teaching to aid its followers in returning to this nature, and so achieve harmony and enlightenment.

Return to the primal nature means overcoming the illusion of separation, resulting from conditioning. This conditioned thinking describes a closed system, where instinct and ego employ rational thought, to create this viewpoint of separation.

The Taoists considered that a clear philosophy was required to transcend this muddled thinking, and that it must be founded on Reality. Anything that was of the world was necessarily a part of the illusion, and so the foundation of Reality must be outside of this.

The Tao produces the One; One produces two (yin and yang); the two produce the ten thousand things. (*Tao Te Ching* ch.42)

Tao therefore is the unchanging, the invariable, which cannot be destroyed. It is the first principle of being from which all things are produced – it is Oneness without form. In producing Oneness it is the Supreme Oneness i.e. beyond Oneness. The Tao, being an invariable, was the only Reality; all things were subject to change. As all of these things originated from the Tao, it was perceived that the law of change was an unchanging law. This is what is really meant by the law of nature.

Being originates in non-being, all else originates from being. (ch.40)

In speaking of LaoTse, Chuang Tsu wrote:
...he made humility and receptivity his outward

expression.

Though he knew the masculine he retained the feminine.

What this means is that the masculine can only be found through the feminine.

(An interesting parallel is in the Taoist exercise of T'ai Ji Quan, where the form is practised to achieve a yielding (i.e. yin) condition. The purpose of which is to allow the free passage of yang.)

Regarding the many paradoxes Lao Tse writes:

When words are true they appear to mean their opposite.

This meaning only that uncommon knowledge, or the wisdom of the sage, comes from knowing the Tao, not from that knowledge which is based on illusion. Therefore knowing that one finds the masculine through the feminine appears as a paradox, but in reality refers to intuitive or unconscious knowledge.

When the Tao is unclear, it is because of illusion or a closed system of thought. One such system appears through the delusion that man is his own judge: that he is capable of formulating a code of morals based on his own limited viewpoint.

Remembering that the nature of illusion is that it appears as reality, disagreeing or agreeing with the point of view is delusory.

Chuang Tsu says of this:

The sage is illuminated by Heaven and so does not

follow.

This means that the Path to follow is that of indifference and through this to achieve freedom from the world. Freedom from the world means, knowing that all things are good and all viewpoints right, despite diversity.

This condition of indifference applies regarding life and death and emotional preference.

The primary consequence of such an attitude is a total acceptance of fate.

BIBLIOGRAPHY

I Ching The Richard Wilhelm translation.
Routledge and Kegan Paul, London 1951.

T'ai Chi and I Ching by Da Liu.
Arkana Penguin Books, London 1972.

The Dancing Wu Li Masters by Gary Zukav.
Fontana/Collins, USA 1979.

The Spirit of Chinese Philosophy by Fung Yu-Lan.
Translation by ER Hughes. Kegan Paul, London 1947.

The Taoist I Ching Translated by Thomas Cleary.
Shambala, Boston and London 1986.

Understanding Oriental Philosophy by James K
Feibleman. Horizon press, New York 1976.